The World of Moths

In the same series

The World of Butterflies
The World of Shells
The World of Minerals

The world of
MOTHS

Michael Dickens

Photographs
by
Eric Storey

Osprey

I dedicate this book to my parents—it is only with their invaluable support and encouragement that I am in my present position as owner of the Butterfly Farm. I hope that their inspiration will enable both myself and my wife to fulfil our joint ambitions for the conservation of butterflies, moths and British wild-life.

M.C.D.

Published in 1974 by
Osprey Publishing Limited,
P.O.Box 25, 707 Oxford Road,
Reading, Berkshire

ISBN 0 85045 164 7

Filmset and printed Offset Litho in England by
Cox and Wyman Ltd., London, Fakenham and Reading

Preface

Maybe you know some people who never read the preface of a book. If so, please tell them that this preface is *not* padding used to fill up the requisite number of pages. It is a plea from both the author and photographer to all of you to enjoy butterflies and moths. You would not have bought this book if you do not share our mutual interest in butterflies and moths. We would like to think that this will fire each of you to think of conserving some of nature's most wonderful of gifts, which are free to those who search for them. General world trends seem to be pointing to a situation where more people will have more time for leisure pursuits. Natural history is more popular than ever before, and it is up to every one of us to protect wild-life. Here we should not forget the insects, especially butterflies and moths, that are so easily pushed out in the so-called progress of civilization. There is, of course, a great need for more land for housing, industrial development and farming, but the world would surely be a poor place without natural things. Most countries are now beginning to become concerned about the protection of their own wild fauna. There is rarely any financial gain involved in doing this, and it will be the amateur who in the end makes things happen. By joining together in a common cause, a number of people can eventually make their ideals work.

We feel that any interest in butterflies and moths is a good thing, and we feel especially strongly that more use should be made of them in education. A child who never sees and learns about them is at a serious disadvantage. If he learns about them when he is young, then some of this knowledge must stay with him in later years, when he will be able to understand the need for conservation. Government bodies, zoos and societies all play their part in conservation, and the Butterfly Farm in particular is in an ideal position to help to provide a service in the fields of education and conservation. We have produced this book in the hope that you will both enjoy it and share our aims for the future of butterflies and moths. It will be obvious, when you read this book, that information on some aspects of the subject is missing; this is good, as it must make everyone realize how much more we need to know if we are to help butterflies and moths to survive.

Acknowledgements

I have liberally borrowed information from many well-known sources when preparing this book, and have been greatly helped by numerous persons. All specimens used for the photographs (with a few exceptions) are in the reference collection of *the* Butterfly Farm. These were either bred at the Farm or obtained from suppliers all over the world.

Particularly sad was the death, a few days before publication of *The World of Butterflies*, of Mr. A. M. Morley of Folkestone, Kent. He would be pleased to know that I owe much to his volumes of Seitz's *Macrolepidoptera of the World* in this book and the previous one (*The World of Butterflies*, published in 1972 by Osprey in England and by Macmillan in the U.S.A.).

The British Museum of Natural History gave me much help, both from their library and regarding classification of moths, and I would like to thank Robert Williams, both for the loan of specimens not in my collection and also for his support with pen and paper. He is one of the few people who knows how much work goes into making a relatively short text! My thanks also to David Boucher for the loan of a specimen.

I would also like to thank my secretary for painstakingly typing all the text, and especially my wife for putting up with my papers and books everywhere while I was researching this book, and for her constant encouragement. I also hope that clients of the Butterfly Farm will feel that this book was worth waiting for, as its preparation has meant a delay in producing price-lists, a job that I always do personally.

Contents

COSSIDAE
1 *Cossus cossus*
ZYGAENIDAE
2 *Cadphises moorei*
3 *Hystiaea amazonica*
4 *Erasmia sanguiflua*
5 *Erasmia pulchella*
6 *Euchromia formosa*
URANIIDAE
7 *Nyctalemon patroclus*
8 *Alcidis zodiaca*
9 *Urania leilus*
10 *Urania ripheus*
SEMATURIDAE
11 *Sematura lunus*
ENDROMIDAE
12 *Endromis versicolora*
LASIOCAMPIDAE
13 *Gastropacha quercifolia*
14 *Lasiocampa quercus*
BRAHMAEIDAE
15 *Brahmaea wallichii*
SATURNIIDAE
16 *Loepa katinka*

17 *Loepa newara*
18 *Loxolomia serpentina*
19 *Heliconisa pagensteckeri*
20 *Dirphia multicolor*
21 *Arsenura armida*
22 *Arsenura aspasia*
23 *Machaerosema mortii*
24 *Eudaemonia derceto*
25 *Dysdaemonia platydesmia*
26 *Automeris illustris*
27 *Automeris aurantiaca*
28 *Automeris grammivora*
29 *Attacus atlas*
30 *Attacus edwardsi*
31 *Rothschildia jacobaeae*
32 *Rothschildia orizaba*
33 *Philosamia cynthia*
34 *Antheraea pernyi*
35 *Antheraea paphia*
36 *Antheraea polyphemus*
37 *Pseudantheraea arnobia*
38 *Argema mittrei*
39 *Graëllsia isabellae*
40 *Actias selene*

41 Eacles imperialis
42 Citheronia laocoon
43 Neocarnegia basirei
44 Aglia tau
45 Saturnia pavonia
46 Bunaea alcinoe
47 Pseudobunaea irius
48 Lobobunaea phaedusa
49 Imbrasia macrothryris
50 Pseudimbrasia deyrollei
51 Cricula andrei
52 Hyalophora cecropia
53 Hyalophora gloveri
54 Dictyoploca simla
   SPHINGIDAE
55 Eumorpha anchemola
56 Eumorpha fasciata
57 Eumorpha satellitia
58 Eumorpha labruscae
59 Manduca rustica
60 Megacorma obliqua
61 Oxyambulyx substrigilis
62 Callionima parce
63 Pachylia ficus
64 Macroglossum stellatarum
65 Hemaris fuciformis
66 Hyles euphorbiae
67 Hyles gallii
68 Deilephila elpenor
69 Deilephila porcellus
70 Deilephila nerii
71 Deilephila hypothous
72 Pseudosphinx tetrio
73 Hippotion celerio

74 Agrius convolvuli
75 Protambulyx strigilis
76 Euchloron megaera
77 Cocytius beelzebuth
78 Cocytius antaeus
79 Acherontia atropos
80 Mimas tiliae
81 Hyloicus pinastri
82 Smerinthus ocellata
83 Sphinx ligustri
84 Amblypterus gannascus
   NOTODONTIDAE
85 Cerura vinula
   ARCTIIDAE
86 Tyria jacobaeae
87 Agyrtidia uranophila
88 Euplagia quadripunctaria
89 Callimorpha dominula
90 Arctia villica
91 Arctia caja
   NOCTUIDAE
92 Bena prasinana
93 Noctua fimbriata
94 Polychrysia moneta
95 Scoliopteryx libatrix
96 Pseudoips fagana
97 Diachrysia chrysitis
98 Catocala sponsa
99 Catocala fraxini
100 Catocala nupta
101 Thysania zenobia
102 Thysania agrippina
    EPICOPEIDAE
103 Epicopeia polydora

Introduction

LIFE-HISTORY OF THE MOTH

The life-cycle of a moth (or butterfly) is surely one of nature's miracles. To develop from an often unattractive larva, through a pupa to an adult moth, is truly remarkable. Let us examine the four stages of this development more closely. I have put the proper scientific terms, singular and plural, in brackets: 1 the egg (*ovum* and *ova*); 2 the caterpillar (*larva* and *larvae*); 3 the *pupa (pupae)*; 4 the adult (*imago* and *imagines*). In stage 3, note that butterfly pupae should be referred to as *chrysalids*, and where the moth pupa is enclosed in silk it is called a *cocoon*.

1 **Ovum** The ovum is laid by the imago and is usually affixed to a leaf of the foodplant. The ovum will *hatch* in one to two weeks, less in the tropics and may take up to six months if it is the winter or *hibernating* stage. Some species may drop their ova in flight and others hide them in cracks in tree trunks. They may be laid singly or in numbers, locally, or spread over a wide area. Normally mating must take place if the ova are to prove fertile, but parthenogenesis is not unknown (where no male is needed—as in certain well-known Stick Insects).

2 **Larva** Frequently the larva's first meal is its own egg-shell. Many larvae only feed at night and, apart from changing their skins three to five times, they appear to do nothing but eat and grow. Most larvae eat a wide mixture of different leaves, but some will only accept a very few. There are also some species that eat things besides leaves. Development takes from one to three months and is quickest in the tropics. If this is the hibernating stage, larvae will take up to nine months to reach maturity. There are some species that spend two winters or more as the larva, but these are few. It is interesting to note the different colours, patterns and decorations of larvae. These often alter each time the non-elastic skin is discarded to reveal a new one beneath. Larvae which are not likely to be eaten by

other creatures are usually brightly coloured and rarely hide, but most types remain carefully camouflaged with patterns that blend into the surroundings. Some have poisonous hairs (e.g. most *Automeris* Saturniid moths), and others resemble twigs or other creatures to gain protection. When fully grown the larva is ready to discard its final skin and reveal the pupa.

3 **Pupa** Larvae that feed on leaves have only to crawl to the ground and burrow, where they form a hollow in which to pupate. Most underground pupae are brown in colour and are quite plain in appearance. There are also silk spinning larvae which attach themselves to a leaf or stem on a pad of silk (but never with a silken girdle as butterflies do). A large number of Silkmoth larvae spin incredible cocoons of silk around themselves amongst the foliage of a tree, or on the surface of the ground (a few types seem too lazy to actually make a cocoon and pupate on the ground). Cocoons always blend in perfectly with their surroundings and the actual construction, colour and thickness vary so much that a species can often be identified from the cocoon alone. Some moths may make a cocoon of chewed-up bark or may utilize any convenient debris. In the tropics, the pupae stage is never dormant, but this is the most likely hibernating stage for moths in cooler regions, thus protection is vital. It is within the pupa that the most fantastic change of all the stages takes place. The cells must break down and completely re-form into the moth within the pupa. How this is done is not really understood. Some kind of complicated chemical process takes place and, just as interesting, is the fact that the pupa must have a built-in 'clock' to be able to hatch at the correct time of year. When ready to emerge the moth can often be seen through the pupa shell.

4 **Imago** The pupa splits and the fully formed moth emerges to expand its wings. Tough cocoons have to be forced open and the moth has a special gland in the adult that secretes a fluid to soften the cocoon. The moth then must crawl up a stalk, force its way through the ground or remain on the outside of the cocoon to expand or, more literally, inflate the wings, which are tiny on *emergence*. This is done by pumping fluid from the body through the veins into the wings themselves and finally the wings must be allowed to dry before the imago can fly. This can take from one to at least six hours. This stage is very dangerous to the insect that has little protection other than camouflage against a predator. Some adult moths will fly immediately their wings are dried, but most night-flying species do not move until after dark, and very often the female will not move until after mating.

It is well known that all butterflies feed on nectar in the imago stage and the same will apply to many moths. However, many moths, especially Saturniidae, do not have a proboscis and are thus unable to feed. It is surely remarkable that these moths can live for up to several weeks without any food other than that stored up since their larval stage.

The life-span of the imago moth varies considerably, from about a week to three weeks on average in the tropics, and up to a year, if the imago stage happens to be the hibernating stage.

I can only generalize in this life-cycle summary and it should be obvious that the entire cycle will happen very much more quickly in the tropics than in temperate regions of the world. Some species will breed all year round, but in cooler regions there is generally only a single cycle and, more rarely, two to three cycles per season. Hibernation is not known in the tropics, but there may be a type of season geared to the rains or the dry periods where nature sees to it that most species will breed when there is plenty of foodplant available.

REARING MOTHS IN CAPTIVITY

For those of you who are interested in doing more than gazing on dead moths, there is every opportunity to breed almost all species. They are nearly always much easier to raise in captivity than are the far more fussy butterflies. The conditions required for raising butterflies need to be far more carefully controlled. The drawback is that for a great many of the species known to collectors, nothing has been recorded about their habits, requirements and larval foodplants. I hope that this book will encourage future collectors to become interested in breeding their captures and to keep records, which are as vital as supplies of living material.

The basic rule for breeding in captivity is to try to reproduce the conditions that would be found in the wild. Sunlight, night and day, temperature, humidity and foodplants are the basic factors involved. Given a species from any place, one can find out some of the answers by reference to meteorological tables. This information, plus notes on foodplants from suppliers, can be nearly all that is required. Most larvae are fortunately not too fussy in choice of diet and alternatives seem fairly easy to find by trial and error. There is virtually no danger of poisoning as larvae invariably refuse to eat any food that would do them harm.

As my next book is to be devoted entirely to the subject of raising species (*How to Breed Butterflies and Moths*), I think only a summary of the principles are needed in this book. I use the word 'natural' to refer to conditions as found in the wild state.

Starting with *pupae*, the stage where most beginners acquire stocks, these will either be non-dormant, when they should be put on peat or soil in an emerging cage at natural temperature and sprayed with warm water several times a day, but very lightly; or, if they are hibernating, the pupae should be put into open trays for the rest of the winter and placed in cool conditions, and no spraying is necessary. In the spring, usually March or April, bring the stored pupae into room temperature, put into a cage and spray when the weather is at all warm, more frequently if it is hot. Cocoons can be hung up by threading-up and hanging-down in strings. Take care to avoid putting the thread through the exit end of the cocoon, instead insert slightly round to the side of the top end. Cocoons may then be thoroughly soaked and kept hot for most successful emergence. Loose pupae should never be allowed to get too wet or too dry and correct spraying comes with practice. Temperature should be as natural as possible, exotics would need 80°–90°F, temperates 55°–65°F, but this could be less without danger. A constant temperature is most important in my opinion. Humidity in the tropics is often 90° saturated, but control is less critical for temperate species. Cocoons hung up do very well in closed-in, steam bath type of conditions.

On emergence, the conditions required for mating the *imago* vary from species to species. But always the natural environment is the answer. Heated glasshouses can be useful, but are apt to become too hot in the daytime. Try to provide a means for the air to circulate naturally, but not violently. Make your cages large for giant species—it is a good idea to allow moths to emerge, fly and mate in one large cage—or, equally good, place inside the large cage a smaller one with the imagines: this avoids handling live specimens. Ensure changes of night to day are visible to the moths, so never use a windowless room. Some species must be paired off into individual cages, but it is not necessary to discuss special conditions now. Your cage can be wood framed, or as supplied by dealers (these naturally will be smaller types). I have found that home-made wood cages are excellent and that nylon, terylene or cotton netting is the best material for covering the cages, as this allows in light, heat and air and is good for observation or spraying purposes. The only drawback to wood is that the cage has to be burnt if infected with disease, whereas metal and plastics can be sterilized and netting covers replaced. Never use closed-in cylinder cages, except where all condensation can be avoided.

Mating of moths may last 1 to 24 hours, depending on the species. Day-flying moths usually mate briefly, as do butterflies, emerging, mating and laying in one day. Ova may be deposited absolutely anywhere or, less generally, only on the foodplant. Most moth ova are quite tough and it is not difficult to scrape them off netting or wood and put them into a plastic box. The advantage of ova laid on food is that they can be left alone to hatch. Do not forget that many moths feed from nectar (not Saturniidae). See if the imago has a proboscis and, if so, provide plenty of flowers or it will die very quickly.

Ova if loose should be put in a closed plastic box, on a piece of plain paper, kept very slightly moist and the date of laying noted. Keep at natural temperature and only add a little water spray if the atmosphere dries. If you spray too much mould will form. Hatching may take as little as a week, usually two weeks, and of course this stage can be for the winter when ova should be kept cool (45°F approximately) in the box and not sprayed.

Larvae: When the young larvae hatch, always transfer to a second box on to clean, dry foodplant. Change food and paper and clean box daily, minimize old food and replace larvae still on twigs and they will walk across on to the fresh leaves themselves. Use larger boxes as they grow and never touch a larva that is skin changing (i.e. when it is hunched up on or off food and looks sick, but is in fact waiting for the skin to burst). As soon as it is large enough not to get out, place in a cage on potted or cut food in water. Continue regular cleaning out and changing food —this is made easier by only giving the amount per day that will be consumed—until the larvae are ready to pupate. Larvae wander around base of cage and many change colours, Saturniidae start to spin cocoons, all indicating the next change. Those that want to burrow should be given several inches of peat, soil or pupating mixture. Saturniidae will generally spin a cocoon in the foliage or on the cage sides. Those types that are to over-winter in this stage can be cooled-off and stored, either as they are, or the pupae dug-up and the cocoons cut off, still on stalks or pulled off netting. Those to emerge very shortly after pupation will need to be kept at natural temperature and dampened. Specimens bred for release in the wild may be set free in any stage, but the two best stages are as larvae or imagines.

STRUCTURE AND SENSES

This discussion only outlines a few important features of moths. Read the section in *The World of Butterflies*, or technical books for more detailed and scientific matter.

Moths have no internal solid structures. They protect their vital organs with a substance called chitin (best known as the hard covering of beetles). Moths cannot carry much weight or

15

they could not fly. Moths (like butterflies) can taste, see, breathe by diffusion, have a simple heart and blood system, a primitive digestive system and various sense organs not known in man.

Proboscis Those imagines that feed have a *proboscis*, or tongue, used to suck up nectar, water or other juices. Even in the non-feeding groups there is present a rudimentary, if useless proboscis. When not in use, this organ is coiled up under the head.

Antennae or feelers are perhaps the most important part of a moth's structure. They have many tiny branches with sense glands to detect odours. Female moths have glands producing scents and males can detect this scent and locate their mate. It is remarkable that the male can detect from all other airborne scents and impurities the scent of his mate, and with two antennae he can actually track her. Many species will *assemble*—the female, if wild, or placed in a cage in the open, will attract males from every direction. I have attracted wild male *Saturnia pavonia* from nearly four miles. This may be luck, but distances of at least one mile in favourable conditions are quite common. This is an excellent method of introducing wild into bred stock. The detailed structure of the antennae varies in virtually every species and is an important factor in their identification. In many species the males have much larger antennae than females and it is this larger surface area that gives them greater powers to detect scents which, incidentally, are rarely perceptible to humans. All moths have either filamentous antennae, pectinate antennae (feathered), or, rarely, broadened at the end, but never actually clubbed as in all butterflies.

Wings The wings of moths are supported by veins and on emergence fluid is pumped into the veins to inflate the wings. When they have expanded, dried out, and the two membranes of the wings have fused together, the moth will then be able to fly. The wing or vein pattern called *venation* varies in every species and this is another main factor in their classification. Fore wings and hind wings of all butterflies and moths are held together during flight by several types of 'hook and pin'. In fact butterflies have a mechanism different to most moths and this is the main reason for placing them in a different superfamily.

Genitalia: Mating in moths is by straightforward sexual intercourse as in higher animals. The genitalia are always slightly different in structure from species to species and this is yet another major factor in identification. It is necessary, however, to dissect the abdomen to be able to examine these organs. Much valuable scientific work is at present being carried out that will differentiate species and identify members of the same species whose many forms may have been confused in the past.

LIGHT TRAPS AND LAMPS

Since it has been discovered that most moths come to light, much work has been done to develop a trap to catch species for sampling or other purposes. Moths are attracted to light through a very complicated and not yet fully understood reaction. It would appear that they fly towards a light, reach a point where they would normally be repelled and, seemingly, become dazzled by the light and fly beyond this point directly into the light source. The most effective lamp is one producing light of short wave length (ultra-violet), invisible to humans, but one tends to use a lamp producing additional visible light.

The actual trap consists of a lamp set in vanes over a funnel leading to a rest chamber. As most ultra-violet lamps require special electrical fittings, they do tend to be rather expensive initially. One can also obtain lamps that can be placed on a white sheet or near a wall, but then one must catch the moths with a net. The advantage of the above traps is that nothing is ever killed. Specimens that have been caught automatically are rarely damaged and may be released again the next day.

EDUCATION AND CONSERVATION

I have already discussed some aspects of these subjects earlier in the book and here only mention the practical side of these considerations.

To be able to help conserve butterflies and moths requires at least a basic understanding of their life-history and this aspect has already been examined. In the past, it was always popular to go out to catch and kill moths purely for acquisition and with little thought for the future. Luckily this trend is now vanishing and people want to be able to observe, photograph and breed moths at home. This is a step towards conserving species. There are many societies and trusts concerned in preserving nearly all wild-life. Taking specimens from the wild should only be done either where it is vital to further study or for the purpose of obtaining breeding stocks. In my own business, we try only to take materials that can be bred and a larger proportion put back into the wild than were originally taken. This depends entirely on co-operation with suppliers and it is to be regretted that so many catchers in foreign countries (and U.K.) are only interested in immediate profit and show no interest in trying to breed what they find. With a little practice and understanding they could multiply their catch many times, return a large number from where they came and still have a saleable 'surplus'. I for one will never cease trying to persuade all suppliers to do just this.

You may ask, why sell them at all? I would say that without supplies of living and even dead butterflies and moths being available, then interest would quickly disappear. Every school should encourage this interest and they must have suppliers of live materials. It is for butterfly farms to meet these demands, as they alone have the knowledge and experience to provide such materials. An interest established through a school when a child is young, will frequently continue in later life.

Development of land for domestic, industrial or farming purposes can be planned to include the preservation of land for all wild-life, but this will happen only if sufficient people want it. Get enough people interested and working together with practical plans, then the matter can be taken to the highest levels before it is too late. I may well be over-pessimistic and possibly have set my ideals too high on the question of conservation but I hope that the necessary support will come.

One does not want to see butterflies and moths entirely reduced to a life of captivity, but a controlled wild state would seem to be the answer. Luckily, the protection of animals and birds, for whom much is already being done, does generally mean the protection of areas of land where insects breed, so the work has already started. The establishment of sponsored research and breeding stations in all areas of the world would be a main objective in the protection of butterflies and moths. I and many others would like to provide these, and I have written this book partly with just such ideas in mind. I always feel it necessary to interest as many people as possible in the fascinating hobby of Lepidoptera in which everyone can play a part. I would like to hear from anyone who thinks he or his organization could help translate some of these ideas into reality.

CLASSIFICATION OF MOTHS (AND BUTTERFLIES)

Any system that is linear in arrangement and thus has to break up species into groups or families with common factors can never be strictly accurate. Thus it is that no definitive layout is ever likely to be made of the classification of Lepidoptera. One cannot show the relationship of one family to another or how close one species is to the next. Thus it is that the usual systems show general divisions into suborders and further into families with the most primitive types first on the list and the more recently evolved types later. It is interesting to note that the earliest lepidoptera came on to this earth immediately before man.

Classification has already been mentioned in passing and the following are the main items used in classification: wing venation, antennae structure, genitalia, the complete life-history as well as obvious external similarities. Add to this the detailed examination of all structures and organs, and even of chemicals within the insect and we may be getting close to accurate classification. Everything possible has to be considered before any real conclusions can be produced, and these are frequently altered as man develops new techniques. The earliest serious attempt at the classification of butterflies and moths was from Linnaeus in the eighteenth century. I have shown below the most modern layout for all butterfly and moth families, after that of I. F. Common, the well-known Australian expert. Note that butterflies occupy but a small section within the many families of moths. I hesitate to use this system, but it is now accepted. I am only afraid that the species illustrated in this book may not entirely conform to this layout! Brief explanations are given after the table:

THE LEPIDOPTERA

ORDER: LEPIDOPTERA
Suborder: ZEUGLOPTERA
Superfamily: *MICROPTERIGOIDEA*
Family: 1 Micropterigidae
Suborder: DACHNONYPHA
Superfamily: *ERIOCRANIOIDEA*
Families: 2 Eriocraniidae
3 Neopseustidae
4 Mnesarchaeidae
Suborder: MONOTRYSIA
Superfamily: *HEPIALOIDEA*
Families: 5 Prototheoridae
6 Palaeosetidae
7 Hepialidae
Superfamily: *NEPTICULOIDEA*
Families: 8 Nepticulidae
9 Opostegidae
Superfamily: *INCURVARIOIDEA*
Families: 10 Incurvariidae
11 Prodoxidae
12 Heliozelidae
13 Tischeriidae

Suborder: DITRYSIA
Superfamily: *COSSIDEA*
Families: 14 Cossidae
15 Metarbelidae
Superfamily: *TORTRICOIDEA*
Families: 16 Tortricidae
17 Phaloniidae
Superfamily: *TINEOIDEA*
Families: 18 Pseudarbelidae
19 Arrhenophanidae
20 Psychidae
21 Tineidae
22 Lyonetiidae
23 Phyllocnistidae
24 Gracillariidae
Superfamily: *YPONOMEUTOIDEA*
Families: 25 Aegeriidae
26 Glyphipterigidae
27 Douglasiidae
28 Heliodinidae
29 Yponomeutidae
30 Epermeniidae

19

THE LEPIDOPTERA (Continued)

Superfamily: GELECHIOIDEA
Families: 31 Coleophoridae
32 Agonoxenidae
33 Elachistidae
34 Scythridae
35 Stathmopodidae
36 Oecophoridae
37 Ethmiidae
38 Timyridae
39 Cosmopterigidae
40 Metachandidae
41 Anomologidae
42 Pterolonchidae
43 Blastobasidae
44 Xyloryctidae
45 Stenomidae
46 Gelechiidae
47 Physoptilidae
48 Strepsimanidae
Superfamily: COPROMORPHOIDEA
Families: 49 Copromorphidae
50 Alucitidae
51 Carposinidae
Superfamily: CASTNIOIDEA
Family: 52 Castniidae
Superfamily: ZYGAENOIDEA
Families: 53 Heterogynidae
54 Zygaenidae
55 Chrysopolomidae
56 Megalopygidae
57 Cyclotornidae
58 Epipyropidae
59 Limacodidae
Superfamily: PYRALOIDEA
Families: 60 Hyblaeidae
61 Thyrididae
62 Tineodidae
63 Oxychirotidae
64 Pyralidae
Superfamily: PTEROPHOROIDEA
Families: 65 Pterophoridae
Superfamily: HESPERIODEA
Families: 66 Hesperiidae
67 Megathymidae

Superfamily: PAPILIONOIDEA
Families: 68 Papilionidae
69 Pieridae
70 Nymphalidae
71 Libytheidae
72 Lycaenidae
Superfamily: GEOMETROIDEA
Families: 73 Drepanidae
74 Thyatiridae
75 Geometridae
76 Uraniidae
77 Epiplemidae
78 Axiidae
79 Sematuridae
Superfamily: CALLIDULOIDEA
Families: 80 Callidulidae
81 Pterothysanidae
Superfamily: BOMBYCOIDEA
Families: 82 Endromidae
83 Lasiocampidae
84 Anthelidae
85 Eupterotidae
86 Lacosomidae
87 Bombycidae
88 Lemoniidae
89 Brahmaeidae
90 Carthaeidae
91 Oxytenidae
92 Cercophanidae
93 Saturniidae
94 Ratardidae
Superfamily: SPHINGOIDEA
Family: 95 Sphingidae
Superfamily: NOTODONTOIDEA
Families: 96 Dioptidae
97 Notodontidae
98 Thyretidae
Superfamily: NOCTUOIDEA
Families: 99 Lymantriidae
100 Arctiidae
101 Amatidae
102 Hypsidae
103 Nolidae
104 Noctuidae
105 Agaristidae

Butterflies will be seen to cover only families 66–72 and of these the 'Skippers' are separate, 66–67. This system puts together under family 70 (Nymphalidae) eight of the families I separated in *The World of Butterflies* (page 12). Moths and butterflies are of the *Order Lepidoptera*. The first divisions are into *superfamilies*, and then into *families*. The further divisions are into *genus* and species (*specific name*). Below this, divisions are rather vague, being into subgenus, subspecies, forms, races, etc. From the table, most of the lower numbered families are of the so-called Microlepidoptera, or tiny moths, but there are well-known larger moths or Macrolepidoptera all mixed up amongst them (viz. families 5–7 and 14–15), thus this old division becomes outdated and confusing. Other people called all moths Heterocera, and butterflies Rhopalocera, but even this division did not hold good, so who knows what is next? A problem arises with those species that have mixed characteristics of butterflies and moths. The use of Latin-type names is simply so they can be made universal. Linnaeus originated the binomial system of naming, that is the genus (generic name) and the specific name (like surname and christian name).

So we have over one hundred families of moths and butterflies, with at least 20,000 species of butterfly named, and probably nearer 1,000,000 moth species, of which at least 50,000 are the larger types.

REGIONS OF THE WORLD

Seitz (*Macrolepidoptera of the World*) divided the world into sections for convenience, partly climatic, partly geographic, and I have found these most useful when discussing range or movement of species, they are as follows:

1 PALAEARCTICA: Europe, Asia, Northern Africa beyond the desert region, from the Arctic to the edge of the tropics. A temperate region that joins the third region in Northern India and Africa.

2 AFRICANA: All of Africa, south of the Sahara Desert, including parts of Arabia and Madagascar, etc. A tropical region.

3 INDO-AUSTRALICA: India, south of the Himalayas and into China, through Malaysia, Japan, Indo-China, Indonesia, New Guinea, Australia to New Zealand, including all islands within the area. Basically tropical except the temperate area in the south.

4 NEARCTICA: Canada to the Arctic and south through North America, south to, but excluding, Mexico. This is a temperate region.

5 NEOTROPICA: Mexico and through Central America and the West Indies to all of South America. Excepting the temperate southern areas, this is basically a tropical region.

Seitz put together 4 and 5 as *Americana*, but it would be better in every way—except size—to unite 1 and 4 as *Holarctica*.

EXPLANATION OF TEXT NOTES

Under each photograph is a summary of the known facts about each species in tabulated form. Of some too little is known, of others too much to give but a general guide in the space available.

Name

As discussed in the section on classification, each is given the generic (genus) and specific name. By quoting the family and the order Lepidoptera one identifies this individual type from all others in the entire animal kingdom.

Sex

A symbol shows the sex of each specimen photographed: ♂ for Male and ♀ for Female. Read together with the section on sexual dimorphism.

Wingspan

Correct wingspan is measured by doubling distance from fore wing tip to a centre line through the thorax. Note: often this span varies from male to female and within a species as indicated.

Range

As only available records can be employed, logical guesswork must also be used to indicate range. A species may be locally common within the range and I have not attempted to divide range into areas of residence or migration.

Habits and habitat

As already noted, it is my hope that future collectors will not only try to breed the moths they catch, but also record as much relevant data as possible. Vegetation, surroundings, climate and habits are all interesting and important. I have given such as I can find of this type of information, but it is often not available and frequently unknown.

Foodplants

Remarks similar to the last also apply here and I have given such information as I can find and noted alternative foods for captive breeding where they are known to me.

Sexual dimorphism

I have confined details to external differences. Genitalia would have to be examined to be certain of sex in some species. This involves dissection and does not fall within the scope of this book.

Variations and similar species

Natural variation is often considerable and I have tried to cover examples most likely to be encountered. I have also noted species similar in appearance and sometimes varieties and forms are mentioned. Note that ground colour refers to the basic or main colouring of a specimen.

1

♀

Scientific name	*Cossus cossus*
Family	Cossidae
Common name	Goat
Wingspan	7·5–9·5 cm.
Range	Throughout Europe, Scandinavia, into North Africa and east into central Asia.
Habits and habitat	Adults emerge in June and July and may be seen resting on tree trunks during the daytime.
Larval foodplants	The larvae are pinkish-red and live in rotting trees. They usually take 3–4 years in developing. It is the smell they emit that gives rise to the common name. Willows and poplars seem preferable but oak, elm, ash and apple are eaten (the wood not the leaves). Can become a pest in orchards.
Sexual dimorphism	The male is only just over half the size of the female, wings more elongated, antennae thicker and the abdomen slimmer with more hair tufts.
Variations and similar species	Some examples may be a light grey colour or very dark, there being several named forms. Similar is the uniformly marked *C. terebra* and several other species.

2

♂

Scientific name	*Cadphises moorei*
Family	Chalcosiinae (Zygaenidae)
Common name	None
Wingspan	7·5–8·0 cm.
Range	Appears to be confined to north India in the region from Sikkim through Bhutan to Assam and Manipur.
Habits and habitat	Rather lazy, day-flying species, that feed from flowerheads or rest on trees with open wings.
Larval foodplants	Not known.
Sexual dimorphism	Sexes very similar, female only identified by large abdomen and slightly finer antennae.
Variations and similar species	Very similar and the only other species in the genus is *C. maculata* (with a yellowish area on the hind wings near the abdomen).

3

♀

Scientific name	*Hystiaea amazonica*
Family	Zygaenidae
Common name	None
Wingspan	6·5–7·0 cm.
Range	Brazil, Bolivia, Peru, Colombia and elsewhere in South America.
Habits and habitat	Day-flying species settling on and feeding from blossoms; however, also coming to light after dark, so may well fly into the evenings. As there is a resemblance to certain wasp species, this may well be an example of protection by mimicry.
Larval foodplants	Nothing known.
Sexual dimorphism	The male is very similar, apart from a very much slimmer abdomen. The fore wings are rather more elongated.
Variations and similar species	There are about twelve rather similar species in the genus, all very distinctive, but not so clearly defined amongst themselves. Very similar is *H. proserpina* with additional red spots on the fore wings.

4

♂

Scientific name	*Erasmia sanguiflua*
Family	Zygaenidae
Common name	None
Wingspan	10 cm.
Range	North India, Burma, Malaysia, Sumatra, Borneo, Java.
Habits and habitat	A day-flying species that can be seen flying in large numbers at lower elevations. Typical of the genus, its long resistance to the cyanide used by collectors is well known.
Larval foodplants	Only known food of the larvae is wild coffee.
Sexual dimorphism	Sexes are very similar only the larger abdomen of the female is outwardly apparent.
Variations and similar species	Variations occur in the amount of blue on the hind wings and in the size and number of the white spots. Similar is *E. aliris*, but this lacks the purplish-brown lines on the fore wings. There are several named subspecies of *E. sanguiflua* from the different areas within its range.

5

♀

Scientific name	*Erasmia pulchella*
Family	Zygaenidae
Common name	None
Wingspan	8·5–9·5 cm.
Range	Found in north-east India, Burma, into China and east to Formosa.
Habits and habitat	This is a day-flying species and apart from often being seen in numbers at lower elevations, little is known.
Larval foodplants	Only food known is wild coffee.
Sexual dimorphism	The sexes are almost identical only being distinguished apart by the slimmer abdomen of the male.
Variations and similar species	In some localities the metallic blue areas are reduced and in others the yellowish-white. Most forms are given subspecific names.

6

♀

Scientific name	*Euchromia formosa*
Family	Zygaenidae
Common name	None
Wingspan	5 cm.
Range	East Africa, Madagascar.
Habits and habitat	Day-flying species feeding on many blossoms. Nothing else known.
Larval foodplants	Convolvulaceae species.
Sexual dimorphism	Males very similar but the abdomen always slimmer and somewhat pointed, with anal hair tufts.
Variations and similar species	There are several species in the genus most being found in the Indian region. Similar is *E. amoena* from East Africa.

7

♂

Scientific name	*Nyctalemon patroclus*
Family	Uraniidae
Common name	None
Wingspan	13–15 cm.
Range	A wide range from India, east into southern China and south through Malaysia, Indonesia and New Guinea, as far as the Solomon Isles.
Habits and habitat	Completely concealed in the daytime with wings wide open, flying in the early evening, especially around flowering trees. In the tropical areas flies all year round, but is quite seasonal in northern regions. (Compare with *Alcidis* that are day-flying.)
Larval foodplants	Unknown.
Sexual dimorphism	The female is rather larger, abdomen broader, antennae a little finer, fore wings squared rather than slightly triangular to the apex as in the male; hind wings with more pronounced and enlarged tails.
Variations and similar species	In the genus are only a few species, but all are rather similar and easily confused. Of the above there are at least six named forms or races, in particular the ground colour varies from buff, golden-brown, to dark brown or even blackish, also the band may be broad or narrow, white to buff, all of which causes considerable confusion within the genus. More work on them is needed. Illustrated is the subspecies *macleayi* (also known as *ssp. goldiei*).

8

♀

Scientific name	*Alcidis zodiaca*
Family	Uraniidae
Common name	None
Wingspan	10–11 cm.
Range	New Guinea and northern Australia (Queensland and New South Wales).
Habits and habitat	Flies during the day, feeding on Lantana blossoms in the sunshine, especially found in river beds or forest edges and also high in the tree tops. Males come to light after dark. Mimicked by the rare *Papilio laglaizei* in New Guinea, thus *Alcidis sp.*, must be distasteful to birds. Often locally very common.
Larval foodplants	Nothing known of its life-history.
Sexual dimorphism	Sexes very similar, abdomen in the male is slimmer and the anal hair tufts are prominent.
Variations and similar species	Very similar is *A. agathrysus* that flies in New Guinea. There are other similar species in the Indo-Australian region.

9

♂

Scientific name	*Urania leilus*
Family	Uraniidae
Common name	None
Wingspan	9–10 cm.
Range	South America, south to southern Brazil and northwards into Central America.
Habits and habitat	Emerging at night, this is a fast, day-flying species fond of drinking at muddy patches on the ground or sitting on foliage. It frequently settles on rocks where it always sits face downwards. Rapid zig-zag flight, often high up.
Larval foodplants	Omphalea sp. (a creeper).
Sexual dimorphism	Females very similar, but rather larger, abdomen larger.
Variations and similar species	This is the best known of eight rather similar species in the genus. *U. fulgens*, a darker form, occurs further north and in the West Indies as does the more angled, smaller *U. sloanus*. Illustrated is the form *amphiclus* with black cross-bands within the pale blue-green on the hind wings that are lacking in type *leilus*—this form is perhaps the most common. *U. sloanus* has red on the hind wings and resembles the species *U. ripheus*.

10

♀

Scientific name	*Urania ripheus*
Family	Uraniidae
Common name	Sunset Moth
Wingspan	8–12 cm.
Range	Only found in Madagascar (Malagasy Republic).
Habits and habitat	Day-flying moth easily mistaken for a Swallowtail butterfly. Glides high over the trees. A guarded secret are its habits in Madagascar. The ova are laid during August in a large mass, the adults emerging in September.
Larval foodplants	Omphalea sp. (Euphorbiaceae family). Mango.
Sexual dimorphism	Males always smaller and otherwise identical except for the much smaller abdomen.
Variations and similar species	(The above also now known as *Chrysiridia madagascariensis.*) Very similar is the East African *U. croesus* in which the rainbow colours all run together.

11

♀

Scientific name	*Sematura lunus*
Family	Sematuridae
Common name	None
Wingspan	9–10 cm.
Range	Central America and the West Indies, south to southern Brazil.
Habits and habitat	Nothing known of the habits.
Larval foodplants	Not known.
Sexual dimorphism	The male of this species is similar, but quite distinct, being of a dark reddish-brown, the main band is ochrous, the tails are shorter and not so broad.
Variations and similar species	This is a genus with only a few species and even these are thoroughly confused. Different, but similar are *S. diana* and *S. aegistus*, but *S. empedocles* and form *selene* seem quite mixed with *S. lunus* as regards classification.

12

♂

Scientific name	*Endromis versicolora*
Family	Endromidae
Common name	Kentish Glory
Wingspan	5–6 cm.
Range	In U.K. a very local species found in Scotland and, more rarely, in southern England. Found in central and northern Europe, north to Lapland and south to Italy, east as far as the Russo–China borderland.
Habits and habitat	The adults emerge in late March or April and may have spent two or more years in the cocoon stage. The males are strong fliers in the bright sun, but the females only move after dark and may be used to assemble males. Prefers the open type of woodland or moorland.
Larval foodplants	The larvae feed on birch, alder, sallow, lime, hazel and hornbeam.
Sexual dimorphism	The female is quite unlike her mate, being considerably larger, often almost twice as big, abdomen very large. The wings are similarly marked, but lack the orange-brown colour and are instead buff-grey and whitish on the hind wings. In some examples, the female has additional pink.
Variations and similar species	This family has obvious similarities to the Saturniidae and is perhaps transitional as regards development. *E. versicolora* is the only species in this genus and is hardly likely to be confused with any other. Noted is the fact that its common U.K. name is after a 'Mr. Kent', and not the county.

13

♀

Scientific name	*Gastropacha quercifolia*
Family	Lasiocampidae
Common name	Lappet
Wingspan	7–9 cm.
Range	Throughout Europe (including England), into Asia, through China to Japan.
Habits and habitat	Exhibits superb camouflage when resting wings together over the back and looks exactly like a dried-up leaf. Emerges in June and July, found flying along hedgerows and the males come to light.
Larval foodplants	The larvae feed on Prunus species, apple, sloe (blackthorn), sallow, willow, hawthorn, etc., and hibernate for the winter on twigs, thus being very hard to see.
Sexual dimorphism	The male is always much smaller, the wings being more elongated, the abdomen very much smaller and the antennae slightly thicker.
Variations and similar species	The ground colour varies from light ochrous to a dark brown colour. The northern race *ssp. alnifolia* is almost black. Other forms may be reddish or with a green hue. Some examples may be up to 12 cm. in wingspan. Similar is *G. populifolia* that is a yellowish-brown colour with more slender wings.

14

♂ and ♀

Scientific name	*Lasiocampa quercus*
Family	Lasiocampidae
Common name	Oak Eggar and Northern Eggar
Wingspan	7·5–8·5 cm.
Range	Throughout Europe and almost the entire Palaearctic region excepting extreme south-eastern Europe.
Habits and habitat	The male is a very active day-flying insect. The female drops the ova at night whilst actually in flight. Races vary but generally southern races take one year to complete a cycle, whereas northern races take two years, hibernating first as larvae, then in the cocoon. Adults fly in June and July and the females come to light.
Larval foodplants	Heather (Calluna), hawthorn, bramble, dogwood, ivy and many others.
Sexual dimorphism	Sexes quite different as shown in both size and colouring.
Variations and similar species	There are numerous subspecies and forms of *L. quercus*; in Scotland and Sweden is the form *callunae* (but now introduced over nearly all of Britain). This is basically a darker race. Other forms may be light or dark in colouring with much variation in the markings.

15

♀

Scientific name	*Brahmaea wallichii*
Family	Brahmaeidae
Common name	Owl Moth
Wingspan	14–18 cm.
Range	North-eastern India (Himalayas, Assam) into Burma and China.
Habits and habitat	Found in the sub-tropical forests at low altitudes. The adults fly in the evening. During the day they may be found in full view, resting on the ground or trees with the wings open wide and when disturbed they rock back and forth on their wings, rather than fly away.
Larval foodplants	In captivity foods are privet, lilac and Ailanthus, in the wild, they may well be similar.
Sexual dimorphism	Sexes similarly marked and coloured, the male always smaller in size and especially so is the abdomen, antennae slightly finer, but not so obvious as in Saturniidae.
Variations and similar species	All *Brahmaea* species are found in the Old World. Best known is *B. Japonica*, a small species from Japan, but there are several other rather similar species in the Far East. Very similar to the above is *B. hearseyi*. The *Brahmaea* are in many ways closely related to the Saturniidae.

16

♂

Scientific name	*Loepa katinka*
Family	Saturniidae
Common name	Golden Emperor Silk
Wingspan	9–13 cm.
Range	Northern India and southern China, but extending further into China.
Habits and habitat	Adults emerge in the early evening and fly rather weakly at night, especially the females. Males seem to have rather a short life-span.
Larval foodplants	Vines (Cissus sp.) and creepers (Vitis sp.) and also may take hawthorn in captivity. Larvae have urticating hairs.
Sexual dimorphism	Colouring of sexes identical, females have abdomens slightly larger than males and antennae fractionally slimmer. The main distinction is in the wings that are much more rounded as well as larger than those of the male.
Variations and similar species	From China is the similar *L. damartis*, a light yellow species: compare also with *L. newara*. Most similar is *L. megacore* from Sumatra. Some variation occurs and there are named subspecies within its range.

17

♂

Scientific name	*Loepa newara*
Family	Saturniidae
Common name	None
Wingspan	12–14 cm.
Range	Found in the extreme north of India, Assam, Nepal and surrounding areas.
Habits and habitat	Emerges in November in native countries, the cocoons are formed some 4–8 weeks earlier and in captivity the hibernating ova hatch in late March. Little known of this moth's habits in the wild state.
Larval foodplants	It is interesting to note the very similar cocoon of this species to *L. katinka*—both being pitcher-pot shaped with open top, and green. In captivity it feeds on hawthorn, maple, sycamore, walnut, willow, hornbeam and no doubt many others.
Sexual dimorphism	The female is somewhat larger and has a much larger abdomen than the male, the wings also being considerably rounded and the antennae finer, colouring perhaps lighter.
Variations and similar species	Previously thought a member of the genus *Rhodinia* to which it is similar in colour and shape but without the ochrous ground colour; its similarity to *L. katinka* is so striking that it may yet be reclassified.

18

♂

Scientific name	*Loxolomia serpentina*
Family	Saturniidae
Common name	None
Wingspan	17 cm.
Range	South-eastern Brazil.
Habits and habitat	Nothing known, except species recorded from January to April.
Larval foodplants	Not known.
Sexual dimorphism	So far the female of this species remains entirely undescribed.
Variations and similar species	A solitary species in the genus, closely related to the large group *Arsenura.*

19

♂

Scientific name	*Heliconisa pagensteckeri*
Family	Saturniidae
Common name	None
Wingspan	10–11 cm.
Range	South-east Brazil, Paraguay, Uruguay and Argentina.
Habits and habitat	Females fly during the daytime and drop their ova in a lump into the grass. The wings are covered with black hair-scales on emergence that are dropped in flight.
Larval foodplants	Not known, but must be low-growing plants of a common type.
Sexual dimorphism	The female is similar, but is more reddish in colouring. The wings are rather more darkly scaled, and the antennae are finer.
Variations and similar species	This is the only species in the genus, very close in structure to the *Dirphia*. Rather similar are the much darker *Ithomisa* species.

20

♂

Scientific name	*Dirphia multicolor*
Family	Saturniidae
Common name	None
Wingspan	10–12 cm.
Range	South-east Brazil.
Habits and habitat	Despite all the many species of *Dirphia* that are recorded, nothing is known of their habits.
Larval foodplants	Not known.
Sexual dimorphism	The female is much larger and quite distinct. The fore wings are dark brown with a creamy-white 'harpoon' markings and band, the wide outer band is cream, the hind wings much darker coloured than in the male, antennae finer.
Variations and similar species	This is a very large genus and whilst many species are confused, the above is easily separated by its distinctive markings.

21

♂

Scientific name	*Arsenura armida*
Family	Saturniidae
Common name	None
Wingspan	14–17 cm.
Range	Through South America to southern Brazil, also probably in Central America.
Habits and habitat	Nothing known.
Larval foodplants	Anona sp., Bombax sp., and many others not named.
Sexual dimorphism	Unusual in that the female is more impressive in richer shades of contrasting browns and ochres. Hind wings entirely rounded, antennae very fine, abdomen broader.
Variations and similar species	Very similar is *A. cassandra* that may prove only to be a form or subspecies. This genus is very confused.

22

♂

Scientific name	*Arsenura aspasia*
Family	Saturniidae
Common name	None
Wingspan	17 cm.
Range	Brazil especially (or perhaps only) in the south-east region.
Habits and habitat	Nothing known.
Larval foodplants	Melastanaceae species.
Sexual dimorphism	The female is similar, but wings slightly more rounded, antennae finer.
Variations and similar species	Most similar in the genus is *A. hercules*, but this has short tails and no white line. Similar also is *A. biundulata* and indeed the example illustrated appears to be half-way between *aspasia* and *biundulata*—they may be merely forms of the same species. A large group, very confused, which requires examination.

23

♂

Scientific name	*Machaerosema mortii*
Family	Saturniidae
Common name	None
Wingspan	18–20 cm.
Range	Southern Brazil to Venezuela.
Habits and habitat	Nothing known.
Larval foodplants	Not known.
Sexual dimorphism	The female is smaller and more rounded, but not available for examination.
Variations and similar species	(Previously known as *Rhescyntis martii.*) Similar, but red-brown ground colour is the larger *M. hippodamia*. There are two other named species.

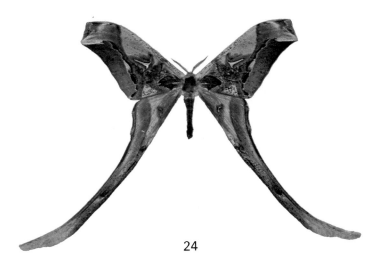

24

♂

Scientific name	*Eudaemonia derceto*
Family	Saturniidae
Common name	None
Wingspan	14–16 cm.
Range	From south-east Brazil to the Guyanas and Venezuela; probably also elsewhere.
Habits and habitat	Believed to be a mountain species. Flies very lazily and is certainly impeded by the long tails.
Larval foodplants	Completely unknown.
Sexual dimorphism	Female not seen, but expected to be similarly marked and coloured, but with shorter and broader tails—note male tails are about 10 cm. long.
Variations and similar species	(Previously *Copiopteryx derceto*.) Compare with examples of the genus form Africana. (Author's note: I cannot entirely agree that this genus should be united with that from Africa.) Several species in the genus are similar, such as *C. sonthonnaxi,* a small dark species, *C. semiramis, C. jehovah* and C. *virgo*, all from South America.

25

♂

Scientific name	*Dysdaemonia platydesmia*
Family	Saturniidae
Common name	None
Wingspan	14–17 cm.
Range	South-eastern Brazil.
Habits and habitat	Unfortunately nothing known at all.
Larval foodplants	Bombax sp., Chorisia sp., but again nothing certain.
Sexual dimorphism	Sexes very similar, but in the female the tails are shorter and usually the ground colour tends to be more ochrous in shade.
Variations and similar species	Illustrated is *ssp. castanea*. Similar are *D. pluto*, *D. kayi* and several other species in the genus. Naming and localities are rather confused. (Author's note: this form is from Costa Rica according to A. Seitz; however, I received the above from Sta. Catarina, Brazil.)

26

♂

Scientific name	*Automeris illustris*
Family	Saturniidae
Common name	None
Wingspan	12–13 cm.
Range	South-eastern Brazil; probably also into Argentina.
Habits and habitat	Nothing known of the habits of this species.
Larval foodplants	Feeds on many trees and shrubs, especially coffee and magnolia and species of Rubiaceae and Melastomaceae, in U.K. probably Acer sp. (sycamore and maple), also Ligustrum sp. (privet).
Sexual dimorphism	Female larger with a darker ground colour, antennae finer, otherwise sexes similar.
Variations and similar species	(Author's note: this example received as *A. illustris*, but even so, does not exactly fit any of the descriptions of species in Seitz—probably a variation.) Compare with *A. coresus, A. banus*, etc.

27

♂

Scientific name	*Automeris aurantiaca*
Family	Saturniidae
Common name	None
Wingspan	5·5–8·0 cm.
Range	South-eastern Brazil; probably elsewhere.
Habits and habitat	Typically of the genus, feigns death if disturbed, dropping to the ground from the resting place.
Larval foodplants	In U.K. bred on lilac (Syringa sp.), cherry (Prunus sp.), willow (Salix sp.), and found to take many foods.
Sexual dimorphism	Female much larger, antennae finer, abdomen broader and similarly marked, perhaps a little paler.
Variations and similar species	Similar is *A. complicata* from this enormous genus.

28

♂

Scientific name	*Automeris grammivora*
Family	Saturniidae
Common name	None
Wingspan	7–8 cm.
Range	Appears to be confined to south-eastern Brazil.
Habits and habitat	Despite being collected for a long time, nothing of the habits seems to have been noted.
Larval foodplants	Probably Quercus sp. (oak), Ceanothus sp. and no doubt many other foods.
Sexual dimorphism	Female similar, but larger and colour duller.
Variations and similar species	This is a very large genus containing around 100 species and many are apt to become confusing (only *A. io* is truly North American). Similar are *A. irene* and *A. metea*, etc.

29

(illustration on facing page)

Scientific name	*Attacus atlas*
Family	Saturniidae
Common name	(Giant) Atlas Silkmoth
Wingspan	15–30 cm.
Range	The various races of *Attacus atlas* extend from northern India (Himalayas) east to Formosa and southwards through all of Indo-China, Malaysia, the Celebes and Philippines to Indonesia, as far as Timor.

29   (*Attacus atlas*)

♂

Habits and habitat	The female does not move until mated and then the flight is most graceful despite the size. The male with his large antennae searches the female at night. In hot regions there are up to three generations in a season, but in cooler areas only a single brood is produced.
Larval foodplants	Few of the *Atlas* group of Silkmoths and the many races have ever been bred, but probably all species require considerable warmth in captivity. Wild foods probably Ailanthus and bamboo, in captivity—we should add a mixture of fruit leaves, willow, sallow, privet, poplar, lilac and rhododendron.
Sexual dimorphism	In all *Atlas*, the male is much smaller than the female, he also has wings more sharply angled in outline and his antennae are very wide compared with those of the female. Some males may be a little darker in colour, but otherwise the sexes are similar.
Variations and similar species	*A. atlas* should be compared with *A. edwardsi*, as perhaps a subspecies. *Atlas* has many named races or geographical forms, from a small red-brown race from Borneo *ssp. manuus* (as illustrated) to the largest moth in the world (that is overall wing area and not wingspan) —*Attacus crameri ssp. lorquinii form caesar* from the Philippines. This name shows that more work is needed on the *Atlas* group, and this race is usually simply named *Attacus lorquinii*. East of Timor, the species is replaced by *Coscinera hercules* in New Guinea and northern Australia.

53

30

♂

Scientific name	*Attacus edwardsi*
Family	Saturniidae
Common name	Edward's, or Himalayan Atlas Silkmoth
Wingspan	20–24 cm.
Range	Found only in northern India in the Himalayan valleys and also in Assam.
Habits and habitat	The adult moth emerges at dawn or sometimes in the afternoon, and due to its large size, may take several hours to expand its wings. The male is very active at night and soon damages his wings searching for his mate, who only flies after mating.
Larval foodplants	Many foods are acceptable to the larvae, the best being Ailanthus (A. glandulosa especially), but will take similar foods to *A. atlas* and will do well on a mixed diet selected from privet, pear, plum and, when larger, poplar or sallow will be eaten. Larvae must be kept very warm in captivity.
Sexual dimorphism	As with all *Atlas*, the female is considerably larger than the male, the abdomen being very fat, the wings more rounded and the antennae finer; otherwise markings and colours are identical.
Variations and similar species	Compare *Attacus atlas*—the same shape and size but the ground colour is red-brown. Nearest to the above is *A. dohertyi* from the Indonesian region. Probably all *Atlas* species originated from a single stock and are thus really all geographical races or climatic forms; although a form of typical *A. atlas* is found in the same areas as *A. edwardsi*.

31

♂

Scientific name	*Rothschildia jacobaeae*
Family	Saturniidae
Common name	Rothschild's Atlas
Wingspan	12–14 cm.
Range	Throughout southern Brazil, Uruguay and Argentina.
Habits and habitat	Despite the fact that it has been reared for many years in captivity, nothing is known of this species.
Larval foodplants	Ligustrum sp. (privet) and Syringa sp. (lilac) in captivity. Wild foods not noted.
Sexual dimorphism	Females always with the wings far more rounded, antennae finer and shorter, abdomen much larger.
Variations and similar species	The only similar species with this ground colour is *R. erycina*, however, the genus is large, rather confused and there are several species of similar shape and markings. Considered to be related to the Asian *Attacus* genus.

32

♀

Scientific name	*Rothschildia orizaba*
Family	Saturniidae
Common name	Orizaba
Wingspan	14–16 cm.
Range	From Mexico and south through Central America and in the west of South America, south as far as Peru.
Habits and habitat	Although it is found almost anywhere, nothing has been noted of this species.
Larval foodplants	Fraxinus sp. (ash), Ligustrum sp. (privet), also cherry, lilac, willow, pepper tree, etc.
Sexual dimorphism	As in all this genus, the males are generally smaller with wings more angled, antennae broader and abdomen always shorter, thinner and with more prominent anal hair tufts.
Variations and similar species	Compare with the very similar *R. speculifer*, *R. jorulla* and the smaller *R. forbesi*. This is a genus with a number of variable species that are most confused in their classification and thus also range. Ground colour varies from bright ochrous to reddish-brown. There are several named races.

33

♂

Scientific name	*Philosamia cynthia*
Family	Saturniidae
Common name	Ailanthus or Tree of Heaven Silk
Wingspan	12–16 cm.
Range	South China was the 'home' of this species now introduced under numerous names to North America and into parts of Europe where it is now resident. Found in India, Malaysia, Indonesia and the Philippines.
Habits and habitat	It will be seen that this very hardy species has quickly adapted itself from tropical to temperate climates. It is easily reared in captivity, although some constantly lose the larvae for no obvious reason. Active after dusk, easily mated, the females lay prolifically. Was used for Eri-silk but proved to be of inferior quality.
Larval foodplants	Ailanthus, privet, lilac and probably plum, willow and numerous other foods.
Sexual dimorphism	Sexes never present any problem as females always have larger abdomens, finer antennae, wings more rounded (especially the fore wings) and are usually larger in size.
Variations and similar species	*P. cynthia* is an example of a species that has been both introduced into new areas and constantly interbred in captivity so that the forms and subspecies have become artificially confusing. That illustrated is as nearly true to type as is available to the author; to list or describe other variations would fill a book! Examples may be brown, olive, reddish, with all manner of marking arrangements and variations in size.

34

♀

Scientific name	*Antheraea pernyi*
Family	Saturniidae
Common name	Chinese Oak Silk
Wingspan	13–15 cm.
Range	(See notes below about artificial range of this species.) Throughout eastern and southern China.
Habits and habitat	Two broods per year, hibernating as the cocoon. However, in captivity can be made to breed continuously. Used commercially for production of Chinese Tussore Silk or Shantung Silk.
Larval foodplants	Oaks (Quercus sp.), sallow, chestnut, apple and other deciduous leaves such as hornbeam, hawthorn, etc. Possibly the easiest of all species to rear in captivity. (Food: Quercus ilex, evergreen oak in winter.)
Sexual dimorphism	Sexes obvious, the males have huge feathered antennae, slim abdomen with anal hair tufts and wings more rounded.
Variations and similar species	The species and subspecies within the genus *Antheraea* are most confused because of their commercial use in sericulture and the numerous artificially bred forms, and because of their introduction into other localities. Thus *A. pernyi* has been recorded from many localities. Similar are *A. yamamai* (Japan), *A. roylei* (Himalayas) and many others. Variation in *A. pernyi* is not great, examples may be plain brown, reddish-brown and with varying amounts of pinkish-red markings.

35

♀

Scientific name	*Antheraea paphia* (= *mylitta*)
Family	Saturniidae
Common name	Tussah (or Tussore) Silk
Wingspan	16–18 cm.
Range	Found throughout India, but commonest in the south, also in Ceylon. (It is not at all clear if similar examples found in Indonesia are subspecies or different species.)
Habits and habitat	Of great importance in the production of silk where the larvae are farmed-out wild on trees, this work continues today, but is now largely for experimental sericulture. Males very active, females sluggish. Probably continuously brooded in the wild, but a single brood in captivity.
Larval foodplants	Feeds wild on numerous foods, such as Ficus and Terminalia, but in captivity prefers oak, beech, hornbeam, or plum.
Sexual dimorphism	The sexes could not possibly be mistaken, the males have enormous feathered antennae and the abdomen is very small compared to the enormous size of the females.
Variations and similar species	Colour varieties are immense within this species from buff, ochre, yellow, brown, red-brown, sepia to almost grey examples. It is almost certain from the hundreds seen that males are never buff and females never reddish in colouring. Considered by some a different species is *A. mylitta* but through years of interbreeding they are now united—this is through silk production of the world-famous Tussah silk.

36

♂

Scientific name	*Antheraea polyphemus*
Family	Saturniidae
Common name	American Oak Silk or Polyphemus
Wingspan	12–16 cm.
Range	Throughout Canada and North America, south into Mexico.
Habits and habitat	One brood in the north, flying May to July, with two in the south, flying February to April and even into July and again from October to December.
Larval foodplants	Many foods eaten, such as Salix sp. (sallow, willow), Alnus sp. (alder), Acer sp. (sycamore, maple), Prunus sp. (cherry, plum, etc.), Crataegus sp. (hawthorn), Quercus sp. (oak), Populus sp. (poplars), Tilia sp. (lime), etc. In U.K. does best on hawthorn, oak, apple and chestnut.
Sexual dimorphism	Sex obvious because of the fine antennae and huge abdomen of the female.
Variations and similar species	A very variable species especially in the ground colour, which varies from bright reddish-brown to pinkish, ochrous, buff and greyish. Size also varies as does the wing outline which may be rounded or rather irregular. Various forms and races are named. There is no other species likely to be confused with the above.

37

♂

Scientific name	*Pseudantheraea arnobia*
Family	Saturniidae
Common name	Buff Emperor
Wingspan	11–13 cm.
Range	Throughout Equatorial Africa.
Habits and habitat	Nothing noted of the habits of this species, except pupae are bright green and covered in short, sharp hairs and not enclosed in a cocoon.
Larval foodplants	Terminalia sp., Uapaca sp. and Poga sp.
Sexual dimorphism	Females always reddish-brown with yellow scaling, markings indistinct. Antennae fine, abdomen large, fore wing apex more rounded.
Variations and similar species	(Also known as *P. discrepans*.) Males may be bright yellow or rather a dull greyish-yellow. Similar to certain *Nudaurelia* sp., and also others in the genus *Pseudantheraea*.

38

♂

Scientific name	*Argema mittrei*
Family	Saturniidae
Common name	Madagascan Moon Silk or Comet
Wingspan	19–22 cm.
Range	Only found in Madagascar (Malagasy Republic).
Habits and habitat	Despite the fact that cocoons are exported the habits of this species appear to be a closely guarded secret.
Larval foodplants	Eugenia and Winmannia? Possibly also on Sclerocarya sp. (marula tree), Commiphora sp. and even walnut.
Sexual dimorphism	Females have tails much shorter and broader, wings larger and more rounded, abdomen larger and antennae much thinner.
Variations and similar species	Ground colour varies from the bright yellow to a pale green yellow, especially in the male. Similar to but larger than *A. mimosa* from East Africa.

39

♂

Scientific name	*Graëllsia isabellae*
Family	Saturniidae
Common name	Spanish Moon
Wingspan	10–12 cm.
Range	Confined to a small region in Spain to the north and east of Madrid.
Habits and habitat	The ova are laid from April to May in the wild but not until June in captivity.
Larval foodplants	Pinus sylvestris, Pinus maritima and, in captivity, on other coniferous trees.
Sexual dimorphism	Sexes similar but the female has narrow antennae, a thicker abdomen and broader tails.
Variations and similar species	Obviously related to the *Actias* genus but quite distinctive and there is nothing similar. Compare also with the genus *Argema* from the Africana region. *G. isabellae* is probably the origin of all other long-tailed Moon-moths and may well have extended further afield in the past.

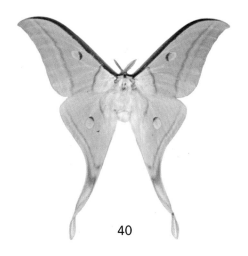

40

♂

Scientific name	*Actias selene*
Family	Saturniidae
Common name	Indian Moon
Wingspan	15–20 cm.
Range	Throughout India and Ceylon, through Indo-China to Borneo and north to Japan, and including Formosa and most of east and southern China including Hong Kong.
Habits and habitat	Number of broods probably depends on locality, in captivity three is usual: the first adults emerge in April, again in mid-summer and lastly in October–November. Quickly damaged, pair easily but are very nervous, mating until dawn.
Larval foodplants	Fruit trees especially mango, juglans, hibiscus and numerous others. In captivity does well on any fruit plus sallow, rhododendron, hawthorn, hornbeam, walnut, etc.
Sexual dimorphism	Sexes very obviously different, the females always much larger in wing area and usually span, wings rounded, abdomen fatter and antennae finer, tails wider and much shorter.
Variations and similar species	Despite its common name this species has numerous forms and races and is found over a wide area. There are several very similar species such as *A. artemis* from Japan and China.

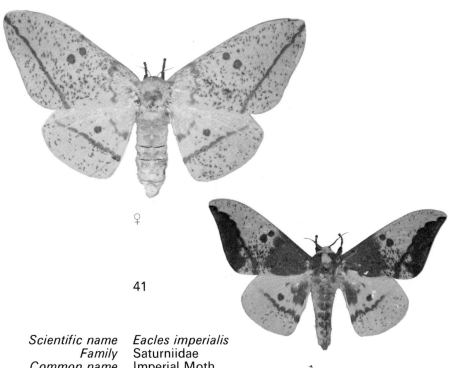

♀

41

♂

Scientific name	*Eacles imperialis*
Family	Saturniidae
Common name	Imperial Moth
Wingspan	11·5–15·0 cm.
Range	Throughout North America, east of the Great Plains, also in Toronto, Canada, and south through Central and South America, as far as southern Brazil.
Habits and habitat	Seems now to be confined to rural areas, flying from June to August in the north, but in the south generally two broods, flying April to July and again from August to November. Comes readily to light.
Larval foodplants	Accepts a very wide variety of foods, such as oak, walnut, hickory, sycamore, maple, sumac, elm, beech, hornbeam, birch, alder, pine, spruce, cedar, cherry, chestnut, privet, etc.
Sexual dimorphism	Quite distinct in every way as illustrated.
Variations and similar species	It seems almost certain, but still waits confirmation, that the above is in fact the same as the North American subspecies and the various forms there and in Central and South America. We have assumed so until further work is done. An extremely variable species, examples being very light or dark and with varying amounts of reddish-brown markings; forms or subspecies named are *oslari, magnifica, decoris, opaca, tucumana, nobilis* and others.

42

♂ and ♀

Scientific name	*Citheronia laocoon*
Family	Saturniidae
Common name	None
Wingspan	9–12 cm.
Range	From Brazil north to the Guyanas and west up to southern Central America; probably also elsewhere.
Habits and habitat	Unfortunately nothing of the habits of this species is known.
Larval foodplants	Possibly cotton (Gossypium sp.), sumac (Rhus sp.), and may well eat walnut.
Sexual dimorphism	Sexes quite distinctly different, as shown—males always much smaller.
Variations and similar species	This genus is closely related to the *Eacles*, but lacks their eye-spots. Varies considerably in the amount of red-brown markings, but no other species has so much yellow on the fore wings. There are roughly twenty others in the genus.

43

♀

Scientific name	*Neocarnegia basirei*
Family	Saturniidae
Common name	None
Wingspan	6·5–10·0 cm.
Range	Southern Brazil only.
Habits and habitat	Nothing known of this species.
Larval foodplants	Nothing known.
Sexual dimorphism	Male quite different in shape, being much smaller, fore wings very angled, concave and pointed, hind wing with a small tail; antennae thicker, body much slimmer, markings and colour similar, except brown tends to be ochrous or pinkish-buff.
Variations and similar species	This is the only species in the genus and there is nothing similar. Genus related to *Syssphinx* group.

44

♂

Scientific name	*Aglia tau*
Family	Saturniidae
Common name	Tau Emperor
Wingspan	6–10 cm.
Range	Central Europe (not in U.K.) and through Asia to Japan. Not found in the Mediterranean area.
Habits and habitat	The males are very active, pairing in the afternoon sun, but the females only move in the evening to lay their ova. Flies from March to June depending on the locality.
Larval foodplants	Beech, oak, birch, lime, sycamore and probably other deciduous trees.
Sexual dimorphism	The female is quite unlike the male, being a uniform pale buff colour with fine antennae, a very large abdomen, and is also nearly twice the size of the male.
Variations and similar species	This is the only species in the genus. Considerably varied, best known is the almost black aberration *ferenigra* with only the inner area of the wings ochrous; also forms may be entirely black or with the marginal band greatly enlarged.

45

♂ and ♀

Scientific name	*Saturnia pavonia*
Family	Saturniidae
Common name	Emperor
Wingspan	6–8 cm.
Range	Throughout all of Europe and into Asia in the north as far as the Russo–Chinese borderland.
Habits and habitat	Emerging in late April or May, the males are very active in the daytime and mate in the early afternoon for less than an hour. The females fly and deposit ova after dark. Particularly common on heathland. Males can find females by scent over several miles.
Larval foodplants	Heather is the principal food in the wild, but will take many others including bramble, sallow, sloe, plum, rose, etc.
Sexual dimorphism	As can be seen from the illustration, the two sexes are quite different in colour as well as antennae and abdomen shape.
Variations and similar species	There are various forms of *E. pavonia* throughout its range, size may vary considerably and colouring also. Males may be ochrous instead of orange or even yellow, and females may be from plain grey-white to having considerable reddish-pink on the wings. Very similar is *S. spini* from eastern Europe in which male and female are both like female *S. pavonia*. Also similar are the much larger *S. pyri* and the darker *E. pyretorum ssp. luctifera*.

46

♂

Scientific name	*Bunaea alcinoe*
Family	Saturniidae
Common name	Common Emperor
Wingspan	12—16 cm.
Range	Throughout Equatorial Africa and south to Natal.
Habits and habitat	Emerges at dusk and mates for only a short period.
Larval foodplants	Celtis sp., Croton sp., Cussonia sp., Ekebergia sp., Maesa sp., Terminalia sp., Gymnosporia sp. and many other foods, including plum and hawthorn in captivity.
Sexual dimorphism	Female antennae thinner and blacker, fore wing rounded, abdomen much broader.
Variations and similar species	Very variable in size and also in colour and markings, several forms named, with the ground colour being reddish, golden, pinkish to dark brown.

47

♂

Scientific name	*Pseudobunaea irius form epithyrena*
Family	Saturniidae
Common name	Irian Emperor
Wingspan	12–14 cm.
Range	Throughout Central Africa and all countries south and east to South Africa.
Habits and habitat	Despite being found over such a large range, nothing is noted of its habits except that males readily come to light and larvae are easily found.
Larval foodplants	Bauhinia sp., Brachystegia spiciformis, Pterocarpus deleroyi, Uapaca nitida, Julbernardia paniculata, etc.
Sexual dimorphism	Females have the fore wing edges straight and not curved as in the male, the antennae always very much finer, abdomen always much larger and without anal hair tufts. Generally the females are the duller colours (greys, browns and buffs, with pinkish markings).
Variations and similar species	As there are no less than seven main forms and numerous subspecies and variations, I have given the name of the above form together with the illustration. Because of all the various forms of this species, many were originally thought to belong to different species. Ground colouring varies from orange-ochrous to pinkish, yellow, pale grey, violet-brown, even red or orange and generally a combination of these colours. There are similar species in the same genus, e.g. *P. tyrrhena.*

48

♂

Scientific name	*Lobobunaea phaedusa*
Family	Saturniidae
Common name	Blotched Emperor
Wingspan	16–20 cm.
Range	In West Africa throughout the equatorial zone.
Habits and habitat	Flies in May, but nothing else known.
Larval foodplants	Probably species of Rhus, Acocanthera, Uapaca, Eugenia, Eucalyptus, etc.
Sexual dimorphism	Females have finer antennae, their wings are more rounded, and their abdomens larger.
Variations and similar species	Ground colour varies from an ochrous-brown to a bluish-brown colour. There are others similar in the same genus such as *L. saturnus*. Compare also with the tailed *Imbrasia* species.

49

♂

Scientific name	*Imbrasia macrothryris*
Family	Saturniidae
Common name	Large-Eyed Emperor
Wingspan	15–16 cm.
Range	Natal to Rhodesia, Malawi, Angola, Zambia to Tanzania.
Habits and habitat	Nothing noted of the habits except that the larvae do not spin a proper cocoon.
Larval foodplants	Julbernardia sp., Brachystegia sp., also on apple and plum.
Sexual dimorphism	Fore wings more rounded in the female, antennae finer, abdomen much broader, also ground colour is brown.
Variations and similar species	There are other similar species in the genus although none so large. Compare also with the genus *Pseudimbrasia*. In some forms the fore wings may be yellowish or reddish.

50

♂

Scientific name	*Pseudimbrasia deyrollei*
Family	Saturniidae
Common name	Giant Emperor
Wingspan	15–19 cm.
Range	Angola, Zambia, Tanzania, Uganda and most of Equatorial West Africa.
Habits and habitat	A forest species but nothing else known.
Larval foodplants	Euphoribiaceae sp., Moraceae sp., Rubiaceae sp., also Erythrophloeum sp.
Sexual dimorphism	The female has much more rounded wings, thinner antennae and the abdomen is much larger. Her wings are also paler with the fore wing spot obviously visible, and the hind wing tail is very blunt.
Variations and similar species	Colour varies from yellow-brown to reddish-brown and plain browns. There are other similar species within the genus.

51

♀

Scientific name	*Cricula andrei*
Family	Saturniidae
Common name	Scarlet-Windowed Silk
Wingspan	7–8 cm.
Range	India, Ceylon and throughout Malaysia and western Indonesia.
Habits and habitat	Two broods in captivity (possibly more in the wild), the first adults emerge in April or May and then again in October. Pairing at night, they part about dawn and are easily disturbed.
Larval foodplants	Many fruit trees are acceptable, in captivity may be reared on these, and also oak, hawthorn, privet, willow, sallow, etc.
Sexual dimorphism	Males almost always smaller, antennae broader and wings more angled, the abdomen slimmer. Colours of male buff to orange-red.
Variations and similar species	(Unnecessarily confused with *C. trifenestrata* that is always reddish, grey-brown colour and has three clear spots on the fore wings.) There is considerable variation in colour and examples of *C. andrei* may be orange-red or even yellowish-buff, particularly in the males, females may be tinged with olive. *C. drepanoides* is similar, but is a dark-coloured species with heavy markings.

52

♀

Scientific name	*Hyalophora cecropia*
Family	Saturniidae
Common name	Robin, or Cecropia
Wingspan	14–16 cm.
Range	Throughout North America, east of the Rocky Mountains, across Canada, south to Mexico and across to Florida.
Habits and habitat	Single brooded, early (April) in the south to June in the far north. Found almost anywhere, even in urban areas. Males readily come to light. Probably hybridizes with similar species, as does so easily in captivity.
Larval foodplants	A great variety of foods, including Acer sp. (maple), Prunus sp. (cherry and plum, etc.), Pyrus sp. (apple), Salix sp. (willow), Syringa sp. (lilac), Fraxinus sp. (ash), Ulmus sp. (elm); best in U.K. are: apple, hawthorn, blackthorn and sycamore.
Sexual dimorphism	Males usually smaller, antennae very much more feathered, abdomen very much smaller and usually ground colour is more greyish.
Variations and similar species	Similar are *H. gloveri, H. columbia* and *H. euryalus*.

53

♂

Scientific name	*Hyalophora gloveri*
Family	Saturniidae
Common name	Glover's Silk
Wingspan	10–14 cm.
Range	Throughout the Rocky Mountain region of North America and Canada, south to Texas, also into Nevada in the west and Dakota in the east, and Manitoba in the north-east.
Habits and habitat	A single brood annually, flying mostly in June, but as early as March in the south, but equally recorded in August (second brood in Texas). Interbreeds with *H. euryalus, H. cecropia*. Although it may be locally profuse, has periods of scarcity in any area, probably due to disease.
Larval foodplants	Willows (Salix sp.), alder (Alnus sp.), wild currant (Ribes sp.), maple, chokeberry (Prunus sp.), buffaloberry (Shepherdia sp.) and larch (Larix sp.); in U.K. larvae are considered fussy feeders.
Sexual dimorphism	Despite colour variation, females unmistakable because of the thin antennae and large abdomen, also generally much larger.
Variations and similar species	This is a most variable species in size, colour and markings. Colour may lack or have additional red, the markings may be very indistinct, the eye-spots large or almost absent and the ground colour may be reddish, brownish or greyish. Several forms and subspecies are named. Very similar is *H. columbia*, also compare with *H. cecropia* and *H. euryalus*.

54

♂

Scientific name	*Dictyoploca simla*
Family	Saturniidae
Common name	None
Wingspan	13·5–16·5 cm.
Range	Confined to the north and north-eastern areas of India into Assam.
Habits and habitat	The adults fly in late autumn and the ova hibernate during the winter.
Larval foodplants	Sallow (Salix sp.), wild pear, apple, walnut. Many other foods suitable in captivity, such as hawthorn and willow.
Sexual dimorphism	The female is perhaps more rounded in wing shape, the abdomen much larger and the antennae thinner, otherwise the sexes are very similar.
Variations and similar species	Very similar to *D. japonica* that may be considered the continuation species found further east into China and Japan. *D. japonica* is less colourful.

55

♂

Scientific name	*Eumorpha anchemola*
Family	Sphingidae
Common name	None
Wingspan	12–15 cm.
Range	From southern Argentina north to Mexico.
Habits and habitat	A vagrant only in North America, feeds from flowers and comes to light. Naturally a very strong flier that wanders afar.
Larval foodplants	Ampelopsis sp. and Cissus (vine).
Sexual dimorphism	Females tend to be even larger than males, antennae finer, abdomen much broader, tip of fore wings rather more rounded.
Variations and similar species	(Previously known as *Pholus anchemolus*.) Similar are *E. triangulum* and *E. pandorus*. In some examples of *E. anchemola* fore wings may be pinkish.

56

♂

Scientific name	*Eumorpha fasciata*
Family	Sphingidae
Common name	Lesser Vine Sphinx
Wingspan	10–11 cm.
Range	From Canada south to southern Argentina.
Habits and habitat	Resident only as far north as Carolina and west to California, further north as a migrant only. In the north there are usually two broods in May to July and August to October, further south it flies all the year round, being continuously brooded. Adults feed at flowers.
Larval foodplants	Vitis sp. (vine), Jussiena sp. (Onagraceae family).
Sexual dimorphism	Sexes very similar, wings more rounded in the female, antennae finer and abdomen broader.
Variations and similar species	Very similar to *H. vitis*, but this species lacks the pink on the hind wing borders. No other similar species.

57

♂

Scientific name	*Eumorpha satellitia*
Family	Sphingidae
Common name	Southern Satellite Sphinx
Wingspan	11–13 cm.
Range	Throughout South America to Argentina and north through Central America and the West Indies, also into Texas.
Habits and habitat	A rare migrant only in North America.
Larval foodplants	Vitis sp. (vine), Ampelopsis sp., Cissus sp. (treebine), also Virginia creeper (Parthenocissus sp.).
Sexual dimorphism	Sexes rather similar except for the finer antennae and larger abdomen in the female.
Variations and similar species	Illustrated is subspecies *posticatus*, the only form with the pretty reddish-pink on the hind wings. Previously this and other subspecies were considered as different species because of the variation. Very similar are other species in the genus, such as *E. anchemola* and *E. pandorus* (with which it was confused in the past).

58

♂

Scientific name	*Eumorpha labruscae*
Family	Sphingidae
Common name	Gaudy Sphinx
Wingspan	12–13 cm.
Range	Really only found in Central and South American countries, but migrates even to Canada; rarely into Argentina.
Habits and habitat	Very much a migratory species, probably flying all seasons in the tropics, but a visitor in the summer and autumn further north and merely a wanderer in the extreme north of its range.
Larval foodplants	Vitis and Cissus sp. (vines), Ampelopsis sp., Eupatorium sp.
Sexual dimorphism	Sexes rather similar, the female has somewhat finer antennae and a larger, more rounded abdomen.
Variations and similar species	Specimens vary especially in the brightness of the colours, but not extensively. There is no other species likely to be confused with the above.

59

♂

Scientific name	*Manduca rustica*
Family	Sphingidae
Common name	Rustic Sphinx
Wingspan	12–14 cm.
Range	Throughout North America except the extreme north, through the West Indies and Central America into all of South America south to Uruguay.
Habits and habitat	Found as a vagrant in northern U.S.A., resident only to Virginia. Appears in North America from May to October and is probably continuously brooded in South America. Comes to light and also feeds from flowers, especially petunia and moonflowers.
Larval foodplants	Chionanthus sp. (fringe bush), Bignonia sp., Jasminum sp. (jasmine), and other foods.
Sexual dimorphism	Sexes very similar, the female has slightly thinner antennae and the abdomen is broader with the anal hair tufts less pronounced.
Variations and similar species	Similar is *M. albiplaga* from South America, but not mixed—lacks yellow on abdomen. The ground colour varies from a dark brown to a yellowish-brown, sometimes with more or less white markings on the fore wings.

60

♂

Scientific name	*Megacorma obliqua*
Family	Sphingidae
Common name	None
Wingspan	11–12 cm.
Range	Found throughout India, Ceylon, Burma and Indo-China, Malaysia and perhaps further east to New Guinea.
Habits and habitat	Despite the fact that this species is frequently seen, no-one appears to have kept any record of its habits.
Larval foodplants	Nothing is known of the life-history of this species, but no doubt a wide variety of foods would be accepted.
Sexual dimorphism	The female is identical, except for the larger abdomen that is more rounded and the antennae, as in all Sphingidae, are a little thinner.
Variations and similar species	There are several rather similar species, but few can be mistaken due to the black line on the fore wings in this particular species—the only example in its genus. Most similar is *Meganoton analis*—found to the north and east into China, this species is much darker in ground colour. See front cover illustration for another photograph of this species.

61

♀

Scientific name	*Oxyambulyx substrigilis*
Family	Sphingidae
Common name	None
Wingspan	13–15 cm.
Range	All of India south to Ceylon, east through Burma to Indo-China and south through Malaysia and Indonesia to the Philippines.
Habits and habitat	Adults rest in the daytime with outspread wings on foliage or tree trunks but are very active at night, coming to light.
Larval foodplants	Plumeria.
Sexual dimorphism	Males tend to be rather smaller, abdomen slimmer and antennae slightly thicker and larger.
Variations and similar species	There are several named forms of this species, those that are considered typical have a wider and darker border and the ground colour is a much darker shade, being a dull brown. The illustration is of *O. substrigilis ssp. pryeri* from Malaysia, especially Sumatra and Borneo. As this species is most variable it is easily confused with similar species such as *O. maculifera, O. liturata, O. dohertyi*, etc.

62

♂

Scientific name	*Callionima parce*
Family	Sphingidae
Common name	Silver-Spotted Sphinx
Wingspan	7–8 cm.
Range	South America, south to southern Brazil, in the west to Bolivia, north through the West Indies to Florida, Texas and Arizona.
Habits and habitat	In North America as a vagrant only. Nothing known of its habits.
Larval foodplants	Unknown, but probably a species of Apocynaceae, such as an Ambelania sp.
Sexual dimorphism	The female is very similar, abdomen rather broader and less pointed.
Variations and similar species	Similar are several species in the genus, such as C. ramsdeni, C. innus, C. denticulata and others.

63

♀

Scientific name	*Pachylia ficus*
Family	Sphingidae
Common name	Fig Sphinx
Wingspan	12–15 cm.
Range	Throughout South America to Argentina and north through the West Indies into Florida or Texas.
Habits and habitat	Breeds all year round, visiting U.S.A. only as a vagrant.
Larval foodplants	Ficus sp. (fig), Artocarpus sp.
Sexual dimorphism	Male abdomen anal hair tuft prominent, antennae thicker and always rather smaller in size.
Variations and similar species	Varies from olive-green, through brown to reddish-brown ground colour, hind wings ochrous or yellowish with brown. Similar is *P. syces*, but a rather plain species, lacking the coloured hind wings.

64

♂

Scientific name	*Macroglossum stellatarum*
Family	Sphingidae
Common name	Humming-Bird Hawk
Wingspan	5·5–6·0 cm.
Range	Throughout Europe except the extreme north and virtually the entire Palaearctic region; in U.K. comes as a migrant only.
Habits and habitat	This is very much a wanderer and may be seen during the daytime and early evening hovering to feed from jasmine or tobacco and many other plants. The moth hibernates and there are frequently two broods in the south, flying in June and again from October, but it may be seen in virtually any month depending on the locality.
Larval foodplants	Bedstraw (Galium sp.), Rubia sp., in captivity on goose-grass and clovers (Galium).
Sexual dimorphism	Sexes very similar and hard to determine, but the knob of the antennae is not so enlarged as in the male and the anal hair tufts more prominent in the male.
Variations and similar species	Little variation, some examples may have a much darker ground colouring or a dark fore wing band. There are several rather similar species from all regions, but none from Europe.

65

♂

Scientific name	*Hemaris fuciformis*
Family	Sphingidae
Common name	Broad-Bordered Bee Hawk
Wingspan	5–6 cm.
Range	Europe except the far north, throughout central and northern Asia to Japan, also in Algeria; in England, but not far north.
Habits and habitat	Flies in May to mid-June, especially in the sunshine, and feeds from many blossoms, especially rhododendron and bugle (Ajuga sp.). In warmer localities may have two broods and often in the cooler areas pupae will hibernate for two winters. Covered in greyish-green scales on emergence that fall off on the first flight.
Larval foodplants	Galium sp. (bedstraw) and Lonicera sp. (honeysuckle and woodbine), also on snowberry.
Sexual dimorphism	Sexes very similar, the female has finer antennae and less prominent anal hair tufts to the abdomen.
Variations and similar species	Very similar species found in the Palaearctic and Nearctic regions. Best known in Europe is *H. tityus*, with a very narrow dark border to the wings. Some variation occurs mostly to the border and abdomen colouring. Where double-brooded there is considerable seasonal variation in the adults.

66

♀

Scientific name	*Hyles euphorbiae*
Family	Sphingidae
Common name	Spurge Hawk
Wingspan	7–8 cm.
Range	Throughout central and southern Europe and in North Africa, east across Asia to China. Also introduced into Canada. A rare migrant into U.K.
Habits and habitat	One brood in the north, flying June and July, with two in the south in the spring and again in the autumn. Pupae often lie over for two years.
Larval foodplants	Euphorbia sp. (sea, portland, cypress and petty spurges), will eat vine in captivity.
Sexual dimorphism	Males have much thicker antennae, often larger in size and the abdomen more pointed and slim, otherwise sexes very similar.
Variations and similar species	This species is most variable and many forms have been named. Illustrated is *ab. rubescens*: the type lacks the rosy-pink on the fore wings. Others may be thickly scaled, sometimes with dark grey-brown patches on the fore wings, or the ground colour may be a pale brown. Similar is the larger *H. nicaea* from Spain; compare also with *H. gallii*. There are many other rather similar species in the Palaearctic region. Very variable in size.

67

♀

Scientific name	*Hyles gallii*
Family	Sphingidae
Common name	Bedstraw Hawk
Wingspan	7–8 cm.
Range	Truly Holarctic, northern U.S.A., Canada, Europe and Asia to Japan, through the entire temperate zone; in U.K. a rare migrant but may come in large numbers.
Habits and habitat	Usually flying in August but in some areas double-brooded, flying from May to October depending on locality.
Larval foodplants	Galium sp. (bedstraws), Epilobium sp. (willowherb) and fuchsia, also Godetia sp. and Asperula sp.
Sexual dimorphism	Sexes very similar, the male antennae are rather thicker and longer and the abdomen is slimmer and more pointed.
Variations and similar species	The North American species has been named *ssp. intermedia* and has less red on the hind wings. Other forms may be dark or light in ground colour. Size may vary considerably. There are numerous rather similar species such as *H. euphorbiae*. Compare also with *H. celerio* and *H. lineata*.

68

♀

Scientific name	*Deilephila elpenor*
Family	Sphingidae
Common name	Elephant or Large Elephant Hawk
Wingspan	7 cm.
Range	Throughout Europe, except the north, through Asia to Japan.
Habits and habitat	Fly in May and June from dusk onwards, feeding on blossoms of honeysuckle, valerian and others. Males coming readily to light. In the warmer regions there is a second brood in the autumn.
Larval foodplants	Epilobium sp. (willowherb), also bedstraw (Galium sp.), fuchsia and many others, including vine.
Sexual dimorphism	Males similarly marked but antennae distinctly thicker and larger, and the abdomen is slimmer and pointed.
Variations and similar species	Considerable variation in some localities. Fore wings may be a dull colour, often olive with pale pink; in others the fore wings may be a very bright red-pink. Not likely to be confused with any other species.

69

♀

Scientific name	*Deilephila porcellus*
Family	Sphingidae
Common name	Small Elephant Hawk
Wingspan	5–6 cm.
Range	Throughout Europe to Asia Minor, but not in the extreme north, also in Algeria.
Habits and habitat	Flies from May to July, especially fond of dry areas, feeding at night on dianthus, valerian and honeysuckle blossoms.
Larval foodplants	Galium sp. (bedstraw), Epilobium sp. (willowherb) and Lythrum sp. (loosestrife).
Sexual dimorphism	In the male the antennae are thicker, the abdomen slimmer and more pointed, markings similar.
Variations and similar species	Very variable, the red may be replaced by pink or the whole insect be very dark, even olive-green with pinkish-yellow markings. Some races are very large in size. A very distinctive species.

70

♂

Scientific name	*Deilephila nerii*
Family	Sphingidae
Common name	Oleander Hawk
Wingspan	10–12 cm.
Range	A very widespread and migrant species, found throughout Africa, extending north-east to India and Ceylon, it is known to wander into central Europe and has even been recorded in the United Kingdom.
Habits and habitat	Breeds all the year round in tropical regions, but in temperate areas has two or three broods per year. Migrates to Europe and is usually seen from July to September. A fast flier that feeds from many blossoms, well known for its long migrations.
Larval foodplants	Nerium (oleander) and Vinca (periwinkle), also on gardenia, jasmine and mango.
Sexual dimorphism	Sexes almost identical, the female has finer antennae and the abdomen is larger.
Variations and similar species	In some races, the underside may be a rich orange colour, lacking the green. On the upperside the green varies from light to quite dark and the amount of pink colour varies also. Compare with *D. hypothous*, a much darker species.

71

♂

Scientific name	*Deilephila hypothous*
Family	Sphingidae
Common name	None
Wingspan	10–12 cm.
Range	India, Ceylon and throughout Malaysia and Indonesia, as far as New Guinea and into Australia. Range uncertain as this is a migrant species.
Habits and habitat	A very fast flying species that frequents blossoms to feed, also comes to light. As for *D. nerii*, this species migrates and it is not clear exactly where it may be considered a resident.
Larval foodplants	Cinchona, katechu and probably many other foods.
Sexual dimorphism	Sexes are very similar, the antennae in the female are always finer.
Variations and similar species	Similar in markings (but ground colour much darker) to *D. nerii,* the well-known species from Africa that migrates into Europe and also into southern India.

72

♂

Scientific name	*Pseudosphinx tetrio*
Family	Sphingidae
Common name	Giant Grey Sphinx
Wingspan	13–16 cm.
Range	Throughout South America, south to Paraguay and north through the West Indies to the tip of North America.
Habits and habitat	Only seen as a vagrant in North America. A strong flier found almost anywhere in South America; comes to light.
Larval foodplants	Euphorbiaceae family, such as Plumeria sp., Jasminum sp. (jasmine) and Apocynaceae sp.
Sexual dimorphism	Females are one of the largest of Sphingidae and are much paler than the male, being greyish-white with less clear markings.
Variations and similar species	The only species in the genus and despite similarities, it is unlikely to be mistaken for any other species.

73

♂

Scientific name	*Hippotion celerio*
Family	Sphingidae
Common name	Silver-Striped Hawk
Wingspan	5–8 cm.
Range	A very wide range throughout almost the entire Eastern Hemisphere, excluding the far north. Palaearctica (in U.K. migrant only), Africana and Indo-Australica.
Habits and habitat	Very much a migratory species, appearing in Europe in the autumn, but in the tropics flies all year round.
Larval foodplants	Vitis (grapevine) especially, but also Cissus, Impatiens, Galium (bedstraw), fuchsia, Virginia creeper, arum, rumex, etc.
Sexual dimorphism	Sexes very similar, female antennae finer and shorter, abdomen shorter, less pointed, and hair tufts less obvious.
Variations and similar species	Considerable variation in size and may have a dull pink or a very bright reddish colour to the hind wings. Similar but larger is *H. osirus* from Africa. *H. lineata livornica* is also similar.

74

♂

Scientific name	*Agrius convolvuli*
Family	Sphingidae
Common name	Convolvulus Hawk
Wingspan	10–15 cm.
Range	Central and southern Europe, Africa to Asia in the west and south. Migrates often very far north; frequently seen in U.K.
Habits and habitat	Feeds at flowers especially phlox and tobacco (Nicotiana sp.), during the evening. In tropics flies during the entire summer, but in the north in the spring and again in late summer where it is essentially a migrant species.
Larval foodplants	Convolvulaceae sp. (bindweed in U.K.).
Sexual dimorphism	In the female the fore wings are almost a uniform grey, markings very weak, and the antennae thinner and shorter, abdomen broader and shorter.
Variations and similar species	Compare with *H. cingulatus* from North America that has more pink on the hind wings. Examples from Europe are usually much larger than those from the tropics.

75

♂

Scientific name	*Protambulyx strigilis*
Family	Sphingidae
Common name	None
Wingspan	11–12 cm.
Range	Throughout Central and South America, south to southern Brazil, in the West Indies; also seen in U.S.A.
Habits and habitat	As a vagrant only in Mexico and Florida (seen in July). Attracted to light.
Larval foodplants	Caju (Anacardia sp.), also others in the family, such as anacardium, spandium, erythroxylon and comocladia.
Sexual dimorphism	Sexes very similar, the female has thinner antennae and the fore wings are rather larger and more rounded.
Variations and similar species	Also named is the dark form with reddish-brown fore wings and copper-brown hind wings, subspecies *rubripennis*. Compare with *P. carteri* that might be mistaken for a very faded *P. strigilis*. There are a few other rather similar species within the genus.

76

♀

Scientific name	*Euchloron megaera*
Family	Sphingidae
Common name	Verdant Hawk
Wingspan	11–12 cm.
Range	Throughout Africana region (that is south of the Sahara) and including the Madagascan Islands.
Habits and habitat	Despite being found everywhere, there is nothing noted of its habits.
Larval foodplants	Grapevine and Ampelopsis sp.
Sexual dimorphism	Sexes very similar, markings identical, the male has slightly thicker antennae and an abdomen that is rather slimmer and more pointed.
Variations and similar species	There is nothing very similar, except perhaps the much smaller *Basiothia medea* that has less brown on the hind wings. In some examples there may be considerable marking with orange-brown, especially on the underside hind wings.

77

♀

Scientific name	*Cocytius beelzebuth*
Family	Sphingidae
Common name	None
Wingspan	11·5–12·5 cm.
Range	Throughout South America to southern Brazil and into the southern countries of Central America.
Habits and habitat	Nothing known, except comes to light.
Larval foodplants	Probably feeds on Annona sp.
Sexual dimorphism	Males very similar and rather hard to compare, antennae a little thicker and abdomen more pointed and slimmer.
Variations and similar species	Rather similar to *Neococytius cluentius* that it resembles, but is not marked in bright green.

78

♀

Scientific name	*Cocytius antaeus*
Family	Sphingidae
Common name	Giant Sphinx
Wingspan	15·5–17·5 cm.
Range	Throughout South America to southern Brazil and north through the West Indies into Florida and Texas.
Habits and habitat	A rare visitor only to North America, seen from October to May and in August, thus probably breeds continuously in the tropics. Males very much attracted to light and found commonly in urban areas in Jamaica.
Larval foodplants	The custard or pond apple (Annona sp. especially A. cherimola and A. glabra).
Sexual dimorphism	The male is usually smaller than the female, wings more elongated, abdomen slimmer and more pointed, antennae slightly thicker.
Variations and similar species	Should be combined with subspecies *medor* thought to be the mainland race, a darker form, whilst the type was thought to be the island race from the West Indies. One of the largest of the world's *Sphingidae*.

79

♂

Scientific name	*Acherontia atropos*
Family	Sphingidae
Common name	Death's-Head Hawk
Wingspan	11–14 cm.
Range	Throughout Europe, except the far north, all Africa into the Ethiopian region.
Habits and habitat	Flies at dusk, coming to light. Well known to rob bee-hives for the honey, adults squeak by forcing out air through proboscis. Very much a migratory species especially in northern areas and appears there in May or June. In the south seen from July to October.
Larval foodplants	Potato in U.K. (Solanum sp.), also deadly nightshade (Atropa belladonna), snowberry, tomato, cape gooseberry, cotton, verbena, jasmine, salvia and many others.
Sexual dimorphism	Females larger, abdomen broader and not pointed as in the male, antennae thinner and shorter, markings identical.
Variations and similar species	In some examples the death's-head markings are not clear, or the bands on the hind wings may be reduced or enlarged, even joined, rarely the hind wings are pale yellow. Similar is *A. lachesis*, the darker species from the Far East, and also *A. styx*. Known since 1634 in U.K. and then called the Jasmine Hawk, later the Bee Robber.

80

♀

Scientific name	*Mimas tiliae*
Family	Sphingidae
Common name	Lime Hawk
Wingspan	7–9 cm.
Range	In Europe from England to southern Scandinavia and Russia to Siberia.
Habits and habitat	Adults usually emerge in May and June, resting on trees in the daytime, and males coming to light after dark. Equally common in urban and rural areas.
Larval foodplants	Tilia sp. (lime), Ulmus sp. (elm), also on alder (Alnus) and perhaps birch and hazel.
Sexual dimorphism	A typical female is illustrated, the male is normally smaller and with broader antennae but especially easy to sex as the fore wing spots are very bright green, the border likewise and the ground colour pinkish-white, hind wings bright ochrous.
Variations and similar species	This is a most variable species and there are many forms. Best known are: *ab. transversa*, fore wing spots joined into a band; *ab. brunnea*, ground colour and spots entirely a red-brown; *ab. obsoleta*, entirely without fore wing spots. Much variation in size.

81

♂

Scientific name	*Hyloicus pinastri*
Family	Sphingidae
Common name	Pine Hawk
Wingspan	8–10 cm.
Range	Throughout Europe and Asia to Japan, not in the extreme south; in U.K. only in the southern counties.
Habits and habitat	Flies from April to July (later in the north), resting on tree trunks in the daytime and feeding from blossoms, especially honeysuckle, at night. Pupae often hibernate over two winters. Has been a pest in some pine forests.
Larval foodplants	Scots-pine (Pinus sylvestris) and Norway spruce (Picea excelsa).
Sexual dimorphism	Females very similar, antennae finer and maybe shorter, abdomen broader and less pointed.
Variations and similar species	Considerable variation and several named forms, most commonly met are the very dark, uniform grey specimens, the plain brown examples and those with pale whitish-grey on the fore wings. Size also varies considerably.

82

♀

Scientific name	*Smerinthus ocellata*
Family	Sphingidae
Common name	Eyed Hawk
Wingspan	8–10 cm.
Range	Throughout Europe except the far north to Asia Minor, Siberia and south into the Mediterranean and North Africa.
Habits and habitat	Flies from May to July, mostly June and with a partial second brood in August. Pupae often hibernate for two years. When frightened shows hind wing eyes and rocks back and forth with spread wings to frighten predators.
Larval foodplants	Salix sp. (sallow and willow), apple (Pyrus sp.), poplar and aspen.
Sexual dimorphism	Males with thicker antennae, slimmer abdomens and usually wings more elongated with fore wing curve more pronounced.
Variations and similar species	Not much variation except fore wings may be a brown ground colour, or the hind wings very pale pinkish-white; *ssp. atlanticus* is a large race from North Africa. Similar is *S. planus* from China and Japan. There are several other species similar in most regions especially *Nearctica*.

83

♀

Scientific name	*Sphinx ligustri*
Family	Sphingidae
Common name	Privet Hawk
Wingspan	7–13 cm.
Range	Throughout the entire Palaearctic region.
Habits and habitat	Adults fly in June and July, or from April in the south, visiting flowers in the evening and readily come to light. Pupae frequently hibernate over two winters. Common in urban and rural areas.
Larval foodplants	Ligustrum (privet), Syringa (lilac), Fraxinus (ash), also Spiraea, Viburnum and other foods.
Sexual dimorphism	Males often larger, but always have thicker antennae and slimmer and more pointed abdomens.
Variations and similar species	Rarely hind wings pale or even white, or with pink on the fore wings, but little general variation except in size. Nothing similar in Europe but compare with several Nearctic species (none have the pink).

84

♂

Scientific name	*Amblypterus gannascus*
Family	Sphingidae
Common name	None
Wingspan	10–14 cm.
Range	Throughout Central and South America to southern Brazil, also in the West Indies.
Habits and habitat	A common species found almost anywhere, males come readily to light.
Larval foodplants	Food unknown.
Sexual dimorphism	The female is very similar with the antennae rather finer, the abdomen less pointed and the wings somewhat more rounded.
Variations and similar species	Very variable species, especially where the markings are concerned; in ground colour it is yellowish, reddish, brown or olive-brown. Fore wing band may be wide or narrow or reduced to large spots. One form has pink and yellow hind wings. Several other species in the same genus are similar.

85

♀

Scientific name	*Cerura vinula*
Family	Notodontidae
Common name	Puss
Wingspan	5·5–8·0 cm.
Range	Throughout the entire Palaearctic region.
Habits and habitat	Adults emerge from May until early July, males coming to light. Easily reared and fascinating with long-horned larvae and very hard wood cocoons formed by the larvae, giving perfect winter camouflage and protection.
Larval foodplants	Populus (poplars) and Salix (willows, sallows), also aspen.
Sexual dimorphism	Males always much smaller, antennae thicker, abdomen slimmer, fore wings more whitish and hind wings a clear white (female hind wings appear yellowish when first emerged).
Variations and similar species	Much variation in markings and colour, some races are almost black, others uniform greyish ground colour, several named forms. Similar is *C. erminea* with dark abdomen and very white wings.

86

♀

Scientific name	*Tyria jacobaeae*
Family	Arctiidae
Common name	Cinnabar
Wingspan	4 cm.
Range	Throughout Europe except the far north and into western Asia.
Habits and habitat	Adults are day-flying in late May and June, being especially common on waste ground, old quarries, heathland and fields where the food grows. Males fly late into the evening and will come to light. May be common one year and almost a pest whilst rare in the same locality the following year.
Larval foodplants	Ragwort and other species of Senecio, also groundsel, coltsfoot and other low-growing foods.
Sexual dimorphism	Sexes very similar but the male always has a very much slimmer abdomen.
Variations and similar species	Forms known where the red is replaced by orange-yellow, even pale yellow, sometimes the hind wings are grey, but common variation extends only to a dull pink-red instead of the usual bright colouring.

87

♀

Scientific name	*Agyrtidia uranophila*
Family	Arctiidae
Common name	None
Wingspan	5·5–6·5 cm.
Range	Peru, Bolivia and Brazil.
Habits and habitat	A day-flying species. Nothing else recorded.
Larval foodplants	Completely unknown.
Sexual dimorphism	In the males the abdomen is obviously smaller and slimmer, antennae are slightly thicker and wings rather more elongated.
Variations and similar species	Rather similar to some of the *Isostola* genus, but nothing so large as this species.

88

♀

Scientific name	*Euplagia quadripunctaria*
Family	Arctiidae
Common name	Jersey Tiger
Wingspan	6–7 cm.
Range	Throughout Europe except the north, including the south and west of England, north to Belgium and Holland, east as far as Iran. Migrant examples recorded further north.
Habits and habitat	Adults fly in July and August during the daytime and also at night, coming to light. This species is often very locally prolific; it is the famous species from the Isle of Rhodes that occurs in the 'Butterfly Valley'. Adults feed from many types of flowers.
Larval foodplants	The small larvae hibernate for the winter and feed in the spring until June on many low-growing plants, such as dandelion, nettle, groundsel, plantain, borage, etc., and also oak.
Sexual dimorphism	Sexes similar, the male has a small abdomen with a tuft of hairs on the tip.
Variations and similar species	(Note: previously known as *Callimorpha hera*.) The type is usually considered as that with an orange colour to the hind wing, red is equally common and yellow (*ssp. lutescens*) is not uncommon in some areas. There are several named races, each varying a little. Size can vary considerably, especially amongst bred examples.

89

♂

Scientific name	*Callimorpha dominula*
Family	Arctiidae
Common name	Scarlet Tiger
Wingspan	5·5–6·0 cm.
Range	Throughout Europe except the Arctic region and into Asia Minor; in U.K. found in the southern counties.
Habits and habitat	Adults fly in the sunshine in June to August and the males will assemble to the female. A local species, where it may be very common. Ova are dropped to the ground and the small larvae hibernate. Adults feed from various blossoms.
Larval foodplants	Many low-growing plants are acceptable especially nettle, bramble, sloe, comfrey, but also sallow and plum (Prunus sp.).
Sexual dimorphism	The female has somewhat more rounded wings, antennae finer and abdomen larger and anal hair tufts lacking, also she is often larger in size.
Variations and similar species	Numerous named forms and races. Fore wing spots may be reduced, increased, enlarged or even absent. The black form is *var. nigra*, or, with one spot only, *ab. bimacula*. There is also a form with yellow hind wings, *ab. lutea*. Hind wings may be almost black or with spots virtually absent. Similar is the yellow hind winged *Nicaea longipennis* from the Himalayas and China.

90

♀

Scientific name	*Arctia villica*
Family	Arctiidae
Common name	Cream-Spot Tiger
Wingspan	5·5–7·0 cm.
Range	Central and northern Europe except the Arctic area, south to the Mediterranean and east to western Asia; also in southern counties of England.
Habits and habitat	Flies in May and June with a second brood in captivity only. Rests on foliage during the daytime and the males readily come to light after dark.
Larval foodplants	Many low-growing plants such as dandelion, chickweed, dock, nettle, groundsel, gorse, etc. The larvae hibernate during the winter and feed up from March.
Sexual dimorphism	The male is rather similar but somewhat smaller with broad antennae and abdomen slimmer and not rounded at the end, usually also less reddish.
Variations and similar species	There are several named forms mostly associated with enlargement and sometimes union of the spotting on the fore wings and likewise the blackish spots on the hind wings. The yellow colour may be reddish to a very pale shade. The English form is known as *ssp. britannica.* Similar is *A. flavia.*

91

♂

Scientific name	*Arctia caja*
Family	Arctiidae
Common name	Garden Tiger
Wingspan	8–9 cm.
Range	Throughout the entire Palaearctic region except the extreme south, into the Nearctic region except the extreme south, i.e. Europe, Asia and North America.
Habits and habitat	Adults fly from June to August, larvae hibernate, but there is often a second brood in captivity.
Larval foodplants	Almost any low-growing plants especially dock, dandelion, nettle, dead-nettle, plus privet, sallow, plum, cabbage and numerous others. Larvae in U.K. are the well-known 'Woolly-Bears'.
Sexual dimorphism	Typical females are always larger than males, having thinner antennae and a much broader abdomen, typical hind wing colour is almost orange as opposed to reddish-orange in the male.
Variations and similar species	Infinite variations and forms named, indeed virtually no two examples are ever the same. Commonly varies in either a reduction of brown areas on fore wings and similarly hind wing spots (light-coloured forms), or an increase of these (dark forms). Less common forms, especially bred examples, may be almost black or white on the fore wings and yellow on hind wings.

♀

Scientific name	*Bena prasinana*
Family	Noctuidae
Common name	Green Silver Lines
Wingspan	4·5–5·0 cm.
Range	Throughout Europe, north to Sweden and into western Asia and Asia Minor as far east as Syria.
Habits and habitat	Adults fly in June and July, males come to light, found in wooded areas where the foods grow.
Larval foodplants	Feeds on oak (Quercus sp.) and birch.
Sexual dimorphism	Sexes almost identical although the abdomen in the male is more slender and with slightly broader antennae.
Variations and similar species	(Previously named *H. bicolorana*.) In some examples the fore wings are much paler and the ground colour has a bluish tinge, also the stripes may be a pale yellow colour. From Tunisia there is a smaller and very pale species, *B. africana*.

93

♂

Scientific name	*Noctua fimbriata*
Family	Noctuidae
Common name	Broad-Bordered Yellow Underwing
Wingspan	5·5–6·5 cm.
Range	Throughout Europe, Algeria, Asia Minor and west Asia.
Habits and habitat	Fly June and July, males coming to light, locally common especially in woodland areas.
Larval foodplants	Primrose (Primula sp.), honeysuckle, violet, dock, birch, sallow, bramble, hawthorn, etc.
Sexual dimorphism	Females always have less prominent markings, their antennae are slightly finer and their abdomens rounded.
Variations and similar species	Females vary from orange to reddish-buff, males from red-brown to olive-green. Many forms are just as common as the type. Many similar species, but not so boldly marked in black and ochre.

94

♂

Scientific name	*Polychrysia moneta*
Family	Noctuidae
Common name	Golden Plusia
Wingspan	3·5–4·0 cm.
Range	Throughout Europe (although only in U.K. since 1890), through central and east Asia to northern China.
Habits and habitat	Adults fly in June and July, sometimes again as a second brood in September. Attracted to light and feed from numerous blossoms.
Larval foodplants	Aconitum (monkshood) and Delphinium (larkspur), also sunflower, burdock and other plants.
Sexual dimorphism	Sexes almost identical, the female is usually slightly larger, has thinner antennae and less obvious anal hair tufts.
Variations and similar species	There are named subspecies in which the ground colour is whitish and in one form the golden-brown is almost entirely absent and the colouring is virtually silver.

95

♀

Scientific name	*Scoliopteryx libatrix*
Family	Noctuidae
Common name	Herald
Wingspan	3·5–4·0 cm.
Range	Throughout Europe and Asia as far as Japan, and also throughout the Nearctic region in temperate areas.
Habits and habitat	This species is most likely to be found hibernating in a cellar or other building from January to March, although in fact the adults are alive from July to almost the following summer. Adults are attracted to light and may be found on blossoms.
Larval foodplants	Willows, sallow, poplar.
Sexual dimorphism	The antennae in the male are broader than those of the female, otherwise there is little to distinguish between the sexes.
Variations and similar species	There is much variation in the amount and brightness of the reddish colouring but no similar species.

96

♂

Scientific name	*Pseudoips fagana*
Family	Noctuidae
Common name	Scarce Silver Lines
Wingspan	3–4 cm.
Range	Throughout Europe except in the south, through southern Russia and Asia to Japan.
Habits and habitat	On the wing in June and July in wooded areas, often found sitting on bracken or undergrowth.
Larval foodplants	Many foods are acceptable especially oak, birch, beech and hazelnut.
Sexual dimorphism	In the female the hind wings and abdomen are silky-whitish, also the fore wings show much less of the buff markings than the males.
Variations and similar species	Previously confused with *B. prasinana*. The British example illustrated is *ssp. britannica* with silvery-white bars and less reddish markings than in continental examples. There are several named subspecies, and the most similar species is *P. hongrica*, in which only two bars are clearly visible.

97

♂

Scientific name	*Diachrysia chrysitis*
Family	Noctuidae
Common name	Burnished Brass
Wingspan	4 cm.
Range	Throughout all Europe, through central Asia to Japan.
Habits and habitat	Flies mostly in late July and there may be a second brood in September. Found almost anywhere, especially where there are plenty of flowering weeds.
Larval foodplants	Stinging nettle, burdock and numerous other low-growing plants.
Sexual dimorphism	Sexes very similar, in the female the antennae are slightly thinner and she lacks the prominent hair tufts on the abdomen.
Variations and similar species	The metallic colouring may be brassy colour or greenish and in some examples the fore wing band is completely joined; there are other forms and various similar species.

98

♂

Scientific name	*Catocala sponsa*
Family	Noctuidae
Common name	Dark Crimson Underwing
Wingspan	8 cm.
Range	Throughout Europe (including southern England), into Asia Minor and in Algeria.
Habits and habitat	Flies in July and August, ova laid on trees in bark crevices where they hibernate till the following June.
Larval foodplants	Oaks (Quercus sp.).
Sexual dimorphism	Sexes very similar. Female antennae slightly finer and no anal hair tufts.
Variations and similar species	Compare with *C. nupta* and *C. fraxini*. There are numerous very similar species to *C. sponsa* especially in the Nearctic and Palaearctic regions with hind wings of yellow, red, black, white and orange colouring. The fore wing markings can be very clear or are often darkened. Well known is the species *C. promissa*, a smaller, lighter species from Europe.

99

♂

Scientific name	*Catocala fraxini*
Family	Noctuidae .
Common name	Blue Underwing or Clifton Nonpareil
Wingspan	9–10 cm.
Range	Central Europe (including Kent and Norfolk in England), north to Scandinavia and through temperate Asia to Japan.
Habits and habitat	Adults are found in wooded areas and sit in the daytime on tree trunks or similar, at night they readily come to light, flying mostly in June to August. The ova hibernate during the winter in bark cracks.
Larval foodplants	The larvae feed on poplar, aspen and sometimes ash.
Sexual dimorphism	Sexes very similar, females usually larger than males with larger abdomen and lack the hair tufts of the male.
Variations and similar species	In some examples, the fore wings are quite darkish grey in colour, in others the wings may be quite pale. As with other *Catocala* there are many similar species in the Palaearctic and Nearctic regions. Status in U.K. rather uncertain.

100

♂

Scientific name	*Catocala nupta*
Family	Noctuidae
Common name	Red Underwing
Wingspan	7–9 cm.
Range	Throughout all of Europe (including the southern half of England), through central and northern Asia, to China and Japan.
Habits and habitat	The ova are laid on bark by the females in August and September. There they hibernate for the winter, feeding as larvae from June during night hours. The adults frequently rest during the daytime with open wings (hind wings hidden) on tree trunks or fences.
Larval foodplants	Willow, sallows, poplars (Salix and Populus sp.).
Sexual dimorphism	Sexes very similar, the females tend to be larger in size. The male abdomen has hair tufts that are more distinct than they are in the female.
Variations and similar species	In some examples the fore wings will be darker and in others the hind wings may be a dingy red or even orange-red. There are numerous similar species within this most distinctive genus to be found in Palaearctic and Nearctic regions, with red, blue, black or white hind wings.

101

♂

Scientific name	*Thysania zenobia*
Family	Noctuidae
Common name	None
Wingspan	12–14 cm.
Range	Throughout Central America, the West Indies and South America, south to Argentina.
Habits and habitat	Despite being a very common species, nothing has been recorded of its habits. Recorded as a vagrant in North America (Florida).
Larval foodplants	Not known.
Sexual dimorphism	The female is very similar, but usually smaller, wings rather more rounded and lighter in ground colour.
Variations and similar species	Note that the underside is a beautiful pinkish-red marked with many wavy lines and an overall blue sheen. Compare with *T. agrippina*.

102

♂

Scientific name	*Thysania agrippina*
Family	Noctuidae
Common name	Giant Agrippa
Wingspan	28·5 cm. (illustration)
Range	From Mexico in the north, through Central America and South America to southern Brazil.
Habits and habitat	Rests on tree trunks with open wings during the daytime; appears to be a forest species.
Larval foodplants	Gutta gamba, Carcapuli acosta, and many others not recorded.
Sexual dimorphism	The female is very similar to the male but tends to be lighter in ground colour and is normally larger.
Variations and similar species	The ground colour varies considerably. Compare with the small *T. zenobia*. Examples over 12 in. (20·5 cm.) wingspan have been recorded, but these are unusual. Believed to have the largest wingspan of any known Butterfly or Moth, but should be compared with *Attacus atlas* and certain female *Ornithoptera* (Birdwing Butterflies).

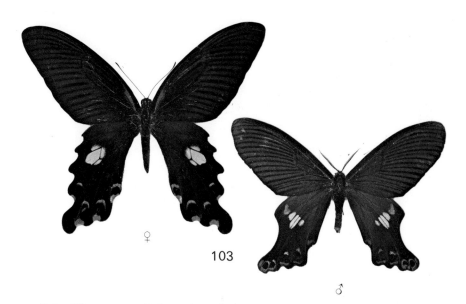

♀

103

♂

Scientific name	*Epicopeia polydora* (+ *Papilio rhetenor* ♀)
Family	Epicopeidae
Common name	None
Wingspan	12–13 cm.
Range	North-west to north-east India and also into Tibet.
Habits and habitat	This species is a mimic of the Swallowtail butterfly *Papilio rhetenor* as illustrated (♀), this is an interesting example of mimetic protection between a butterfly and a day-flying moth. Known to feed from flowers.
Larval foodplants	Unfortunately not known—the larvae are covered in threads of a wax-like secretion and look like a colony of scale insects.
Sexual dimorphism	Differences not noted—it is expected that the female will be larger (maybe as large as the mimic), with the usual finer antennae and broader abdomen.
Variations and similar species	*P. philoxenus* and *P. dasarada* are also butterfly mimics of *E. polydora* but are not as similar to it as is *P. rhetenor*. There are a few other species in the genus that extends from east Asia to Japan and south to Malaysia. Very similar is *E. caroli*, which may even prove to be a subspecies of the above.

COMMON NAMES INDEX
Numerals refer to illustrations, not to pages